THE TIMES

careers & jobs
in the
police service

kim clabby

KOGAN
PAGE

First published in Great Britain in 2004 by Kogan Page Limited
Reprinted 2007

Kogan Page Limited
120 Pentonville Road
London N1 9JN
United Kingdom
www.kogan-page.co.uk

British Library Cataloguing in Publication Data

A CIP record for this book is available from the British Library.

ISBN-10   0 7494 4204 2
ISBN-13   978 0 7494 4204 0

Typeset by Saxon Graphics Ltd, Derby
Printed and bound in Great Britain by Bell & Bain Ltd, Glasgow

Contents

Contents

Foreword

I welcome the opportunity to provide this foreword. It is almost a cliché that 'we live in challenging times' but this has never been more true than it is for the police service now. The challenges being faced by the police continue to grow, as even a quick read of a newspaper on any day of the week would show. Those perpetrating crime are becoming more organised and more sophisticated, demanding increased skills in police officers responding to this challenge.

The very nature of policing is also changing. In the UK, policing is undertaken through the consent of the public. The public, however, are becoming more demanding. The public expect their police to be answerable in the way they go about their business. Greater clarity, improved responsiveness, better efficiency and cost effectiveness... the list goes on. These changes also place pressure on officers, again demanding higher skill levels in leadership and management skills (at all ranks).

A specific issue currently being addressed by police forces throughout the UK is that of racism, in its broadest form. Respect for diversity is seen as an absolutely vital attribute in any potential police officer. Recent TV coverage has highlighted the issues involved, and has spurred police forces to address the issues with urgency. It does not come as a surprise that this book dedicates a whole chapter to these issues. I urge you to regard them seriously.

So, the challenges to be faced are considerable. Meeting them and conquering them is therefore even more satisfying. If you really want to 'make a difference' then there could be no better time to join the police. Mastering the skills required to meet the challenges will equip you with attributes much coveted by employers within and without the police service. Career opportunities are opening up in the wider justice sector, with increased emphasis being placed on multi-agency working and team responses to issues. Rewarding careers are there for the taking – if you can meet the challenge!

Foreword

For those of you reading this book, I wish you good luck. If you decide to join, then I wish you luck in a rewarding career. If you decide not to, good luck too, and I hope that by reading the book you have a better understanding of the police service and how it operates. Either way, I hope you all have a better grasp of the issues involved in policing and what the challenges really are. That surely is a benefit to all of us.

Dick Winterton
Chief Executive
Police Skills & Standards Organisation

Preface

In this country policing has evolved over the centuries into the professional organisation in operation today. It grew from society's need to protect itself from ruthless elements and its main objectives have stayed the same over the years – preventing crime, apprehending criminals and serving the community.

It is one of those controversial professions that invites both praise and criticism in equal measure. The Police Service is justifiably proud of its successes but burdened by its occasional well-publicised failures. The British taxpayers naturally expect and deserve a good professional service from their police officers, and any dents in public confidence are taken very seriously indeed.

So what is life really like in the modern Service? Stressful, dangerous, frustrating – or varied, stimulating and rewarding? Well, it's all of those things. Policing is without doubt a demanding and fulfilling career – not so much a job as a way of life, and the Service tries hard to provide a friendly work environment for all its staff.

Provided the minimum entry requirements are met, fast-track graduates, regular school-leavers and mature career-changers are all encouraged to apply for a job in the police. Whatever the applicants' sexual orientation, ethnic origin, or religious beliefs – the Police Service will take them all into consideration and as a committed equal opportunities employer, treat everybody fairly. The aim is to provide the public with a truly representative body.

The initial selection procedure is tough but fair, and the training rigorous and highly structured. This means that when fully-fledged constables finally emerge from the probation period, they will be well equipped for the challenges ahead. After that, the journey will continue to be a steep personal learning curve – but there will be plenty of support and encouragement along the way.

In the pages that follow, the author draws on over 30 years of hands-on experience to give you an insight into the workings of the modern Service. This seventh edition of the Careers Series is packed with information on selection procedures, training, the rank structure, promotion, conditions of service and career opportunities, as well as hot tips and case histories.

Civilian staff

Police numbers are currently at record levels at over 138,000 – the wider police family of officers and civilian staff now exceeds 200,000. This includes a growing number of Community Support Officers (CSOs) and police staff introduced through the radical police reform programme.

It was Bob Hope who joked 'I hear they are recruiting civilians into the police force now – whatever next'! This comment may have seemed a contradiction in terms 60 years ago, but today it is quite unremarkable. The Police Service is not a military or political organisation – it is a civilian service with a rank and grade structure governed by Act of Parliament. Civilians now account for a sizeable proportion of the total employees and perform a vital role as specialist support staff, freeing up those much-needed patrol officers. Chapter 10 provides information on the requirements and eligibility criteria for civilian support services.

Acknowledgements

I would like to thank the following people for their valued contribution: William Mead, Home Office; Stephanie Hall, Metropolitan Police; Inspector Mark Weaver, Positive Action Team; Wendy Moran, Press Office; The Police Federation of England and Wales; Clive Morris, National Black Police Federation; and all the men and women who provided the case studies.

Introduction

IS THIS THE JOB FOR YOU?

You have to be a special kind of person to become a police officer. From watching films and television programmes, you probably have a picture in your mind of just that person. You may doubt you are made of the 'right stuff', but you are probably wrong – the Service has never been staffed with clones of Wonderwoman and Superman! Despite efforts by the entertainment industry to convey gritty reality, there are still many misconceptions about the job. Glamorous and gung-ho it certainly is not. The reality is a heady mix of action stations and boring bureaucracy, stress and stimulation, frustration and achievement, criticism and praise. Really, what the police are looking for are sensible balanced individuals, able to put everything into perspective and who neither under- nor over-react to unpredictable situations.

Talking about misconceptions, you may be harbouring some now about your eligibility. For example, which statements do you think are true or false?

- you must be able to swim;
- you must be able to drive;
- you cannot join if you wear glasses;
- you must be tall;
- you cannot have a tattoo;
- you must have GCSEs;
- you cannot join if you received a caution as a teenager;
- you must live in the area where you apply.

All of course are *false*. Many of the rules have been relaxed to be more inclusive – although if you specifically wanted to join the Underwater Search Unit, the ability to swim could be rather useful!

The next checklist contains some pertinent questions, which are mainly concerned with your personality and attitude:

1. Are you socially aware?

2. Are you calm and objective in stressful situations?

3. Are you moral, disciplined and self-reliant?

4. Are you logical, with an enquiring mind?

5. Are you willing to take orders?

6. Are you a good team player?

7. Are you genuinely tolerant of people from different backgrounds?

8. Are you capable of presenting written and spoken information clearly?

9. Are you willing to work unsocial hours?

10. Are you confident and assertive?

If you have answered yes to the above 10 points, you really should apply. First though, consult Chapter 1 for the details of the minimum entry requirements, such as age, eyesight, nationality and fitness. Then log on to the Web site of your chosen force and confirm any specific entry-level conditions, because there are slight variations between the Services of England and Wales, Scotland and Northern Ireland. Familiarisation courses are run by most forces and are a good way to test the water first. See Chapter 14 for a list of contact/Web site addresses, which also includes the informative Police Service recruitment site with its 'Could You?' logo. You can write, phone or apply online, and information and recruitment packs will be sent to you on request.

However, there is no magic formula for automatic entry into the police. Every application is judged on its merits, so the more plus points you obtain, the better your chances. There are serving officers with first-class honours degrees, but there are equally many more that have few educational qualifications. Being able to demonstrate previous community work or a Duke of Edinburgh Award will certainly help your application. Involvement in both team and individual sports demonstrates fitness and teamwork, as well as dedication and perseverance.

The skills and personal qualities required to make good police officers are of course very different from those for civilian staff, because of the nature of their roles. Nevertheless, some qualities are expected in all new recruits, whatever job they are applying for. Honesty, stability, intelligence, fairness and common sense are characteristics that are required from everyone who works for the Service. Like any other organisation, the Police Service simply wants the best possible people within its ranks. The tasks are many and varied, so there is a rewarding career path for all those who work hard.

Responsibility

Police officers protect the public and enforce the law. You may have to reassure and support victims or witnesses, while dealing appropriately with the perpetrators. This is a lot to ask of anyone and it is not always easy. It takes an ability to work well with colleagues, cooperating and supporting each other, and developing team spirit.

You must possess a sense of responsibility towards the public and your colleagues, something to sustain you even when you are tired at the end of the day, or are dealing with an unpleasant situation. A bond will be formed with colleagues, so that you rely on each other in difficult circumstances. Your ability to work successfully in a team must be matched by your self-confidence and willingness to take charge of people and situations when you are sometimes on your own. Ask yourself – are you a team leader or a team player? Are you naturally resilient? Have you already held positions of responsibility at, for example, school, college or work?

Confidence

As a representative of authority, a police officer must be confident and assertive. You should have a realistic outlook on life, combined with a steady manner that is neither aggressive nor timid. This kind of confidence generally comes with a wider practical experience of life through work or community involvement. However, it can also be developed by assertiveness training. As a police officer you must always remain calm under pressure, especially when facing the flak (which is quite often). On one day you could be arresting and detaining suspects and gathering evidence, which you will have to present eventually in court. On another day you could be attending a bad traffic accident or fire. On another you could be responding to a frantic call for assistance from a domestic violence victim. And you will frequently have to interview aggressive suspects or traumatised victims and witnesses, in order to establish all the facts – so you cannot be a shrinking violet!

Observation

Excellent observation skills are also important: police officers have to be clear-sighted and alert – a conviction may depend on your accuracy. When you undergo your recruitment tests, you will be marked on how carefully you can observe scenes and how accurately you can record details. Check the eyesight standards in Chapter 1 to make sure you are eligible (though wearing glasses need not be a problem).

Honesty

This goes to the heart of your personality and is a matter of integrity. Nobody's perfect, of course, and most people have told lies at one time or another. But we all know people who make a real habit of it, and they inevitably lose trust and respect.

As a police officer it is important that you are completely straightforward and truthful in your dealings with the public and your fellow officers. In the courtroom, honesty is essential, so as to avoid a miscarriage of justice, bringing the reputation of the police into disrepute, and even (quite rightly) landing you in jail! There will be many occasions when moral courage is just as important as physical courage.

Eligibility

BASIC REQUIREMENTS

A quick eligibility check follows. Remember to confirm specific requirements with your chosen force(s). If you have previously applied to join the police and been rejected, you may retry after six months has elapsed. You can also apply to more than one force at a time, but you will need to list them as first choice, second choice, etc.

Age

The earliest you can send in your application is on your 18th birthday, for appointment at 18½. You can join in your 20s, 30s, 40s, and technically even in your 50s, but since normal retirement is at 55 and there are two years of probationer training, you must be realistic. However, the Service needs a broad mix of age and experience, from the fresh-faced to the battle-hardened, and so welcomes school-leavers and graduates, as well as older applicants looking for a second career.

Nationality

You can apply if you are a British or Commonwealth citizen and, according to the Police Could You? Web site, you can also apply if you are an EC/EEA or foreign national with no restrictions on how long you can stay in the UK.

Height

There are no height restrictions.

Educational qualifications

Applicants should have a good basic educational standard, but generally no formal qualifications are necessary. Check with your local forces for their minimum requirements – there may be regional variations. The assessors will explore your educational achievements, any professional course you have completed, or other study undertaken in your own time.

You will however have to undergo the National Assessment Process (PIRT 3 and 4), which will probably include two written exams, four interactive tests and an interview. The written exams establish whether your command of English is good and that you are numerate (see Appendix 1 for practice tests). You must have the ability to cope with the initial training course and the intellectual capacity to handle the full range of tasks expected of a police officer, including the written work that frequently has to be done as part of your duties.

HOT TIPS

If you are not an academic type, or if English is not your first language, or if you simply hate exams of any sort, you can prepare for the tests by perhaps:

- reading plenty of newspapers and books;
- doing crosswords and number puzzles;
- practising simple arithmetic without a calculator;
- adding up darts scores quickly.

Then to get the best results you should:

- have plenty of sleep the night before;
- be punctual and unhurried on the day of the test;
- remember to take your glasses with you (if you wear them);
- listen carefully to any instructions;
- read each question carefully;
- work quickly but accurately;
- conserve valuable time, not waste it on questions you find impossible;
- answer as many other questions as you can to get the highest score.

Eyesight

If you wear glasses or contact lenses, this will not necessarily disqualify you, but you may have to submit an eyesight report with your application. Your vision must be of a sufficient standard to enable you to do your job properly. The following specifications are taken from the Police Recruitment Web site and are a general guide:

- Unaided vision (without spectacles or lenses)
    - 6/36 or better in either eye (2nd line down on an optician's chart) is required. Binocular vision (vision with both eyes) worse than 6/6 (7th line on chart) requires correction.

- Aided vision (wearing spectacles or lenses)
    - 6/12 or better in either eye (5th line down) and 6/6 or better with both.

- Near vision
    - 6/9 with both eyes together (aided).

- Colour vision
    - Severe colour vision deficiencies (monochromats) are not acceptable. Anomalous trichromats are acceptable. Severe anomalous trichromats or dichromats are acceptable, but you will need to be aware of the deficiency and make appropriate adjustments. The use of colour correcting lenses is not acceptable.

- Corrective eye treatment
    - Applicants will be rejected if they have a history of a detached retina or glaucoma, and if they have undergone Radial Keratotomy (RK), Arcuate Keratotomy, or corneal grafts due to the side effects of these treatments. Applications will be accepted from people who have undergone Photorefractive Keratectomy (PRK), LASIK or LASEK surgery, provided that six months have elapsed since surgery, there are no residual side effects and the other eyesight standards are met.

Tattoos

It used to be that you could not have a tattoo anywhere on your body, but times and fashions change and now that tattoos are commonplace they will no longer disqualify you, provided they are discreet and hidden from view. If they are visible when you are on duty, they obviously must not be the intimidating kind that could cause offence. (If you have dots around your neck with the words 'cut here' – you will be rejected straight away!)

Criminal convictions

Criminal record checks are made on all applicants. In an ideal world, no one who works for the police in any capacity would have a criminal conviction. As a police officer you must respect and uphold the law and have a high standard of personal behaviour and social conduct. However, some very minor offences from your past may not exclude you. You should immediately disclose any caution or minor conviction (usually a juvenile misdemeanour), and it will be investigated. For example, if you were given a caution for minor substance abuse five years previously when you were a teenager, you would probably still be eligible to join the police.

On the other hand, a history of offences that indicates a disregard for the law or society in general will definitely lead to rejection, and if you have been convicted of a serious offence or served a prison sentence, do not even bother to apply. A police officer with criminal associations or a conviction can be vulnerable to pressure to disclose information. Also, an officer's position as a witness in court is undermined, as any conviction has to be declared.

Debt history

A police officer should not be open to corruption, so failure to discharge any debts must be reported straight away. You cannot have any outstanding County Court Judgements or liabilities. Once you have discharged the debt, you may be considered. However, if you are a registered bankrupt, three years have to elapse before you can apply for the police.

Neither you nor any partner may be involved in any outside business activity (for hire or gain) that could compromise your position as a police officer. This includes running a shop, pub or betting office in your force's area. Submit all the details, just in case the police decide that this particular business interest is not likely to cause you, or them, any problems.

Health/fitness

Police work is no stroll in the park, and applicants must be fit enough to perform the basic duties of a constable in a reasonable and safe manner. This involves a degree of strength, agility and stamina in order to use police equipment, defend yourself and others and to deal effectively with public disorder.

You should be in good health, both physically and mentally. A medical officer will examine you to make sure you pass the standards needed for entry into the police. You should be of good general physique, with a satisfactory correlation of height and weight measurements (neither excessively underweight nor overweight for your height). If you have a medical condition, such as asthma, epilepsy, diabetes, cartilage problems or hearing difficulties, it may make you unsuitable to carry out the duties of a police officer. Should you have any doubts about your health, contact your local force for advice before applying.

2

Application and recruitment procedures

VACANCIES

At the time of publication, there are over 8,000 vacancies throughout the Police Service of England and Wales, for example. While not all constabularies have vacancies, most do. Some on the other hand have vacancies, but are not recruiting due to lack of funds.

The time from application to appointment varies from area to area. Some take as little as two months, while others can take a year – the average is around six months. So, it is advisable to check first with your chosen area.

HOW TO APPLY

Either log on to the national recruitment Web site (www.policecouldyou.co.uk) or contact your local force by phone or e-mail and ask for an application pack. You can of course apply to any Police Service you want, not just the one nearest to your home. The question of accommodation, however, will have to be considered carefully. Read through all the information on the relevant Constabulary Web site, which will be updated regularly.

HOT TIPS

Advance planning and preparation are the key to success with your application. The statistics speak for themselves. The police reject about 9 out of 10 applications, and are obviously looking for reasons to reject the majority. You should take the time and trouble to make your application stand out from the crowd. Remember the Police Service operates like a vast business with a written set of rules. Follow the rules and you won't go wrong. For applications submitted by post:

▓ Photocopy the application form in case you make a mistake on the original.

▓ Practise your written answers.

▓ Expand your replies wherever possible and give examples.

▓ Emphasise your strengths.

▓ When satisfied with the draft, fill in the original clearly.

▓ Use black ink/fountain pen if possible.

If you pass through the initial assessment stage you will move on to the next stage of the selection process. Over 2003–4 the Service is phasing in a new assessment and selection procedure that will iron out inconsistencies between forces.

Initial tests

A successful applicant will be asked to attend an assessment centre in order to take tests and be interviewed. This is known as the Police Initial Recruitment Tests (PIRT). The assessment will include:

▓ short written tests including verbal logic and numeracy tests;

▓ group problem solving;

▓ role play;

▓ interviews.

The applicant will receive plenty of information about the tests and assessments before the day. However, practice tests are available and examples of verbal logic and numeracy tests (*How to Pass the Police Recruitment Test* by Harry Tolley, Catherine Tolley, William Hodge; Kogan Page, £9.99, 0749441925; forthcoming) are given in the Appendix.

The interview is your opportunity to shine. Don't worry about appearing nervous, it is to be expected. You should expect some of the questions to be quite confrontational, so be careful not to bite back! Here's some advice:

▨ Rehearse at home in front of a mirror, answering possible questions such as: 'why do you want to join the police' and 'what do your family think about the idea?'

▨ Do your homework well in advance and find out all you can about the force from their Web site and elsewhere.

▨ On interview day, have a neat hairstyle, and wear a suit or plain outfit, white shirt or blouse, black shoes and dark socks.

▨ Don't sit down until invited to do so, then make sure you sit upright.

▨ Look confident and smile.

▨ The interview panel will be sitting a few metres away, so speak up.

▨ Listen carefully to each question and its implications before answering.

▨ Look at all the panel members when replying, not just at the speaker.

▨ At the end of the interview, when asked if there is anything you want to say, do not automatically say 'no'. Could you perhaps add something or make corrections to any of your previous answers?

Do not ask an obvious question, such as how much you will earn, as this information is widely available. If successful you will then be asked to attend a medical and fitness test.

Medical/fitness tests

The fitness test that you will be required to pass consists of three parts:

1. Progressive shuttle run ('bleep test') to measure endurance fitness. You must run between two lines 15 metres apart at an ever-increasing rate. You have to reach four shuttles at level 5 to pass.

2. Testing on a 'Dyno' machine to assess (upper body) dynamic strength. After a warm-up, you must complete five seated chest pushes and five seated chest pulls, with short recovery periods between each exertion. To pass, the average force of the sum of the five pushes must be 34kg, and 35kg for the pulls.

3. Static test for grip strength using a dynamometer. You must achieve a force of 32kg.

Three attempts will be granted to pass the tests, and will be phased over a period of several weeks to allow for improvements after further strength training. The old 'press-up' tests have been replaced with the introduction of the 'Dyno' machine, which is fairer to women, who naturally do not have the same upper body strength as men.

You will probably want to go straight down the gym to train for the test. Remember that prior to starting any fitness programme, it is sensible to seek medical advice. It is also vital to warm up the body with stretching exercises – this will reduce the risk of injury. At the end of any workout, you should cool down in a controlled way, in order to prevent muscle soreness.

HOT TIPS

- Start aerobic sessions gently, build up gradually to at least 30 minutes.

- Space out your exercise – three times a week is best.

- Check your progress and work on improvements.

- Alternate running, cycling, rowing and stepping sessions.

- Set realistic targets.

- Train with a friend to help motivate you.

- Practise your grip strength by crushing/releasing a squash ball.

3

Training

FROM RECRUIT TO CONSTABLE

No one is expected to have any prior knowledge of police work and everyone in training is treated equally, whatever their age or previous background.

The list of topics covered during training is long: the history and social context of policing, the role of the police today, the British legal system, court procedure, human relations awareness and communication skills, specific areas such as vehicle documentation, missing persons and lost property.

There are practical classes on crime with demonstration arrests, court appearance, and charge and bail procedure. You are taught how to use a pocket book, how to give evidence clearly in court, what powers of arrest or search you have in given circumstances. The list is, of course, constantly changing to keep abreast of current trends and new legislation.

A good deal of learning is done with the help of audio-visual aids, particularly video-recording. A mock arrest, interview or trial can be simulated and then analysed and discussed so that you learn by example and by your own mistakes. Role-playing is an essential part of the process. There are written and practical tasks (both individual and group) throughout the training and you are expected to work hard.

Physical skills are also important. The police must know how to move as a disciplined body – important when controlling crowds at sporting events or on peaceful demonstrations, vital when faced with an unruly or hostile mob. There are practical exercises in crowd control to learn how a relatively small number of officers can hold back a much larger gang of people. In recent years more attention has had to be paid to riot shield training and how to cope with an increasing level of violence.

Self-defence is another vital skill that may save your life when you are patrolling alone. You are expected to know how to administer first aid in an emergency and so this too is taught and tested.

Your life will certainly change if you become a police officer and your new career will present many exciting opportunities. One factor you must consider carefully is that you will often be required to work unsocial hours, and this will inevitably disrupt your personal life. You should think about whether your friends and family will be supportive. However, for relaxation you will have a wide choice of sports to help you let off steam. Police officers generally work hard and play hard throughout their careers.

Basic training

Each region has a slightly different training programme, but initially, you will spend a few weeks with your local force, where you will receive your uniform and be sworn in before a local magistrate. Lectures will include details of your particular force, policing and the law. Afterwards you will be required to undergo a residential training course at a Police Training Centre (PTC) or at Centrex, usually for 15 weeks (18 weeks for the Metropolitan Police), with continual assessments, examinations, simulated incidents and self-defence classes. It is a very arduous course.

Most policing skills need to be refined by experience and observation and there is a daunting amount to be absorbed. Some recruits may feel swamped by the demands made on them and the information they have to assimilate. Some drop out early, others do not finish the course, but generally trainers, supervisors and tutors all give huge support and encouragement to overcome any problems that might arise. Because police work is so demanding, it requires a great deal of professional knowledge to be absorbed in quite a short period of time. This is why the training is thorough and meticulously planned to be of the most practical value.

Case Study

Stewart (new recruit – age 20 – training school)

I had my doubts about joining the police. Things like – could I take orders (I even got chucked out of the scouts), could I keep my bottle if a yob spat at me, and could I get up for the early shift after a night out with my girlfriend? The problem was – what I knew about the police only really came from the TV and newspapers – I'd never had a run-in with them myself, though there were several hard cases at school who had! The type of work appealed to me, but I always had niggles about if I'd fit in as the 'new boy' – I'm more the independent type.

As it turns out, training school is no cruise. I'd been a coach down at the local gym after leaving school with two bad A Levels, so I had no worries about the fitness sessions like some of the others, who I've got to say are in pretty poor shape. I was one of three from the same town who started training school on the same day – two lads and one girl – so we all support and moan at each other! But I thought stuff like the role-playing would be easy, just acting, but it isn't – it just shows you up as a bit of an idiot. There's a lot to remember all at once, so you've got to think on your feet. There's loads of rules and regulations, law, etc, to learn, and it seems as if there aren't enough hours in the day. We were all brain-dead on our feet to start with but it's got better as time's gone on and I'm starting to get myself a bit organised.

I can't wait to get out of here and start 'proper' police work down at the local station, which is luckily not far from my digs. At the station I'll have a minder with me all the time – quite a comforting thought – like a dad, or maybe a mum!

Probationer training

Following basic training, you will enjoy a week's leave and then return to your local force, where an experienced tutor constable will guide you through day-to-day policing procedures. You must do a minimum two years' operational training as a probationer.

During these two years you will learn the basics of police work – both in the classroom and out on the streets. You will be helped to develop your skills through study and personal assessment, with constructive feedback from your tutors. It is vital that personal and academic development goes hand in hand with operational experience.

Training at the police station

Having successfully completed your initial training, you will be assigned to a police station. Training in the station is a challenging new experience to cope with. The first few days can be confusing, as you become part of the system. You have to learn the correct procedures, how shifts work, where to go for various activities or supplies, and, of course, you have to meet the colleagues with whom you will be working, who all look so incredibly experienced and competent! Gradually, however, all will become familiar and routine and, as most people will have been through the same process, they will sympathise with you.

Eventually, when you are considered ready, you will be patrolling on your own – stopping and questioning members of the public, giving advice, making arrests and presenting evidence in court. The public will not automatically know that you are a probationer constable (apart from your youthful looks perhaps!). They just see the uniform and expect you to know everything. This on-the-job training is interspersed with further courses to consolidate your increasing fund of knowledge. Gradually you become more experienced and accepted, as you become familiar with the local streets and the local people. You get to know other members of your shift on and off duty. Police procedures and jargon become second nature.

Throughout your probationary period you will be assessed at three- or four-monthly intervals by a sergeant and an inspector who will submit written reports on your progress regularly to senior officers. The sergeant will observe your work on the beat, your performance in court, your judgement and success in making arrests, your ability to write reports, and your attitude towards the public and colleagues at the station. You will then have assessment interviews with your inspector and superintendent. It is very important to maintain a satisfactory standard, both in these reports and at the training classes. This may sound an alarming series of hurdles, but the system is designed to pick up any problems as early as possible.

Finally, at the end of the probationary period, your progress is assessed. If this is judged to be satisfactory, you are then confirmed as a constable and remain in the force. From then on your future career is up to you – promotion and specialisation depend solely on individual merit.

Case Study

Marie (PC – age 33 – two years' service – local station)

I used to be a nurse at a major hospital. All of us there had first-hand experience of the results of violent crime. Night after night the police would bring in blood-covered victims and I would chat with some of the officers about what had happened to the patients. As time went on, I began to think that if I was at the scene of an attack, not only could I give first aid, but I could try and help find the attacker as well. All very noble of course! If I'm honest about it, I was also looking for a better-paid job, but still a vocation like nursing.

So I bit the bullet and applied to my local force without telling anyone. After what seemed ages, but was really only about five months, I was called up for an interview. This went ok and I passed all the tests (though I had to take the fitness test a couple of times to get through). About three months later I started my training. At first I was worried that I would be the oldest in the class, a sort of 'mother hen' to a group of youngsters. But to my surprise, the ages in our group ranged from 19 to 42, so I felt right at home and settled in fine. I was a pretty good student, if I say so myself, and really enjoyed the whole process, except for the self-defence. Probably because of my nursing, I didn't object to the discipline. When I finally went out on to the streets on probation, I felt quite self-conscious. People in the town centre seemed to be looking at me because I was so obviously 'new', but it soon clicked that there is no way to know if a PC has 10 minutes or 10 years service, just by looking at their shiny shoes. Of course the public soon find out when there's a crisis and the thin blue line is flapping in the breeze! There were many instances where I simply had to take a deep breath, try not to panic, and rely on my training. It served me well and now I am a bit more relaxed. I feel really proud of myself and hope that I am making a difference, even if it's only a small one.

Centrex

In 2002 a non-departmental public body called the Central Police Training and Development Authority (Centrex) was created, to provide greater consistency and less duplication in police training. Centrex offers career-long learning with a great choice of specialist courses, and has numerous training centres in England and Wales. It consults closely with Police Services and experts at home and overseas. According to its Web site it also liaises with: the Association of Chief Police Officers, Association of Police Authorities, Police Staff Associations, Police Training and Development Board, Police Leadership Development Board, Police Promotions Examinations Board, Police Skills and Standards Organisation, Police Standards Unit, HM Inspectors of Constabulary, the Home Office, universities, and the private sector. So you can see just how many agencies are at work looking after your career!

Training schedule

To recap, the six training stages are as follows.

Stage 1 (in force, minimum two weeks)

You will obtain a basic understanding of the role of the police officer and learn how to deliver the best service to the public. Some forces extend this period to five weeks and include elements (like a driving course) that most forces cover in stage six.

Stage 2 (at training centre, normally 15 weeks)

The basic core skills will be covered, which will help you deal efficiently with a wide range of operational and everyday situations. *Annual leave* (one week).

Stage 3 (at station, two weeks)

Station procedures will be taught. Then you will start to go out on accompanied patrol and acquaint yourself with the local community.

Stage 4 (on patrol with a tutor constable, 10 weeks)

Under the guidance of a trained tutor constable, you will put into practice everything you have learnt. You will arrest suspects, report offenders, make reports and generally deal with a wide range of everyday police work.

Stage 5 (two weeks)

Your suitability for independent patrol will be assessed and you will learn more about local procedures and policing plans.

Stage 6 (remainder of probation training)

There follows the remainder of your probation leading up to the end of your two years' service, which must include a minimum of 30 days' dedicated training. Your performance will be assessed on a regular basis in terms of competence, skills and knowledge, and you will need to complete a portfolio, showing you have completed all the tasks expected of a police officer. Confirmation in the rank of constable is followed by a massive celebration! *Annual leave* is taken at appropriate stages during the two years.

ON CONFIRMATION AS CONSTABLE

Fingerprints and DNA

You will be required to have your fingerprints taken and a record will be kept for elimination purposes only. A DNA sample will also be retained on a separate database.

Police Attestation Oath

By the time you have been confirmed and taken the following oath, you will be aware that being an officer is much more than simply doing a job of work. You will be following a very demanding career. Both on duty and off, it will affect your way of life. The oath is:

I do solemnly and sincerely declare and affirm that I will well and truly serve Our Sovereign Lady The Queen in the office of Constable, without favour or affection, malice or ill will, and that I will to the best of my power cause the peace to be kept and preserved; and prevent all offences against the persons and properties of Her Majesty's subjects; and that while I continue to hold the said office I will, to the best of my skills and knowledge, discharge all the duties thereof faithfully and according to the law.

4

Through the ranks

CAREER OPPORTUNITIES

Being a police constable offers good earnings and career progression. It is one of the few careers where you are constantly learning and facing new challenges. In many professions, your success is measured by how far up the corporate ladder you climb. Within the Service many police officers choose to stay at the rank of constable throughout their entire career – a measure of how fulfilling and rewarding the role can be. It gives them the chance to stay in touch with the public and be involved with front-line policing all the time.

However, if you wish to diversify from the role of constable, you could move sideways into almost any branch of the Service. There may be opportunities for you to transfer to short-term posts, allowing you to try your hand in different specialist areas and begin to establish career development plans.

No one will pretend that it is easy to move into a specialist role. Competition is fierce and selection is made purely on ability, your record as a constable and your suitability for the role in question. For details of the Police High Potential Development Scheme (HPDS) and other routes to specialist roles see Chapter 5.

THE INITIAL RANKS

Constable

The current rank structure has not varied a great deal (apart from adding sub-divisions to the higher ranks) since the introduction of Peel's New Police. Generally speaking, the police officer the public is most likely to encounter is still the uniformed constable. This could either be a response officer who is first to the scene of a crime or incident, or a neighbourhood patrol officer who has been given the responsibility of a particular locality and who has become an integral part of the community.

As a constable you will help your team provide 24-hour cover, which involves working nights, early morning and late shifts. You soon find out that you are spending the majority of your time at the 'sharp end'! Of course, the higher up the rank structure you go in the police, the more you will become involved in supervision and administration, which necessarily entails more time safely back at the station or behind a desk doing paperwork.

Often as an officer on patrol you will notice the unusual and bring to light offences that might otherwise have gone undetected. Even when working alone, you will keep in close radio contact with your station. You may simply want to pass on information or ask for some facts to be checked, but if there is a problem you can ask for immediate assistance, and be reassured – it will be rapidly provided. While it is the CID officer who takes over the investigation of serious crime, it is in fact the uniformed constable who initially receives most crime reports, so you will often become involved in interviewing offenders and putting the initial paperwork together. You may also be called upon to assist with searches, crowd control or house-to-house inquiries during major investigations.

After incidents, there are inevitably numerous statements to be taken, forms to be completed and reports to be written back at the police station. It may be a crumb of comfort for you to learn that there are strenuous efforts being made behind the scenes to try to reduce the time you spend every day processing paperwork. Just don't expect miracles!

Your uniform and equipment are provided free of charge. When you leave the Service, you are obliged to return all items.

Case Study

Lisa (WPC – age 26 – three years' service – crime squad)

I applied to the Police Service while still at university, based on my predicted 2.1. Two of my friends did the same but they weren't so lucky. I could easily have gone for the graduate entry scheme, but after a lot of discussion with the Force and a friend who's already in the job, I applied in the normal way. I wanted to see what it was like first and knew I could always try for the normal promotion process later on. Now the scheme's changed anyway and there are different rules. Anyway, like most students at uni, I'd had it up to the eyeballs with round-the-clock cramming and exams. Having seen a fair bit of the country through my geography field course trips, I didn't feel I could go back to living at home with my parents, much as I love them, so accommodation was going to be a problem, whatever job I did. Rents now are so high, especially in London, and buying a flat completely out of my reach, even if I shared with someone else. However, as a police officer I've at least got a chance, what with a good starting pay in the Met plus all the various allowances. At the moment I am in a flat-share with three others and my rent is manageable, so I hope to save a bit for the day when I'll be able to afford a place of my own. By then my basic pay will have been boosted by a few increments, so it will be a much rosier situation financially.

Training and probation passed by in a flash and was surprisingly enjoyable. The camaraderie was great – they're a real fun crowd. After I did my 'time' I had to patrol some difficult areas. It's surprising how people can retain a sense of humour in among burnt-out vehicles and piles of garbage! Not everyone comes up and talks to you of course. There's a few cat-calls and this general atmosphere of suspicion that you can sense as you walk around. After that I jumped at the chance to join the crime squad and I'm in my element at the moment – out of uniform for a while (and loving that), and hiding behind net curtains and sitting in greasy white vans watching known villains. I have had to interview several suspects, though I think I was given the easy ones because I'm the new girl. No results as yet, but it's only a matter of time. It's Lord Lucan or nothing! The bonus of this particular squad is that there's very little paperwork for me to do, thank goodness. All my colleagues are resigned to the never-ending process of filling in forms and tapping info into the computer. You'd imagine that with an army of civilians helping out, there would be no need for police officers to get involved with red tape.

Sergeant

A police sergeant is on the first rung of the management ladder and responsible for supervising uniformed constables on the shift, who will be constantly looking for help and advice. There is usually more than one sergeant on duty (three or four in the larger stations under the supervision of an inspector). You may be based either in the station as custody officer, outside patrolling on foot, or in a police vehicle.

You must make sure that the constables are performing their various duties correctly and give them assistance if they need it, or personally deal with any unusual or potentially difficult incident that might arise. In addition, you must check all reports, paperwork and correspondence completed by the constables in the course of their duty (prior to double-checking by the inspector). In addition, you must supervise probationers, make recommendations about them, and be able to answer any of their questions on points of law. A sound knowledge of the local force is essential.

It is possible for standard entrants to become sergeants within five years, subject to passing national qualifying exams and then succeeding through the assessment process.

The exam is in two parts. Part 1 tests your knowledge of criminal law and procedures; Part 2 sets a series of work-simulation exercises, to determine if you have the necessary skills to perform at a higher rank.

Inspector

Promotion to inspector is via an exam and an assessment process, but promotion to ranks above inspector is based on selection only – there are no qualifying examinations. Senior officers in the Police Service need to be able to undertake a variety of specialist roles, including leading and managing people, taking control of incidents and handling complex policing issues and – of great importance nowadays – managing budgets.

As inspector, you are personally responsible for whatever happens during the hours your particular shift is on duty. Should one of the constables or sergeants get involved in a difficult or potentially dangerous situation, then it is up to you to sort it out. Both the activities in the station and out on the beats have to be supervised by the inspector, as well as incidents such as fatal road traffic accidents or serious personal injury. Other duties include organising and supervising the policing of small local parades or public order events (such as demonstrations).

Management, particularly staff management, is what your rank is all about. Internal discipline, career, welfare matters and forward planning all land on your desk. In addition, you must keep abreast of new legislation and case law, so that authoritative advice can be given.

The special procedures and structure relating to each particular force must become second nature, because there is an enormous amount of internal paperwork to be dealt with. The local area must be well researched, especially its crime trends, its problem families, and its potential trouble spots. Also, you should keep close contact with outside organisations via representatives such as social workers, probation officers, housing officials, doctors, nurses, youth club workers and local journalists. In addition, it is your task to give written annual assessments on junior officers, as well as doing probationers' reports. It is on your personal recommendation that members of the shift are put forward for consideration for specialist work.

THE UPPER RANKS

The next rungs of the ladder include chief inspector, superintendent and chief superintendent. Beyond this the rank structure differs in London from the constabularies. In the Metropolitan Police, the upper ranks range from commander, deputy assistant commissioner, assistant commissioner, deputy commissioner, to the head of the force – the commissioner. (A commissioner also heads the City of London Police.) In the constabularies the ranks are assistant chief constable, deputy chief constable, and at the top – the chief constable.

Chief constables are responsible for the management of policing in their area. To keep policing in tune with local needs, the areas are broken down into divisions, each under the control of a superintendent. The divisional headquarters controls a network of stations. Home beat crime prevention, and other community officers work from individual police stations that also have their own Criminal Investigation Department (CID), police cells and communication centres.

Though the forces naturally maintain close contact with one another, each enjoys local autonomy under its own chief constable, who has the authority and responsibility for policy-making within his or her own particular area and reports to the local Police Authority, made up of local people, councillors and magistrates. This does not, however, mean that the police are completely at the beck and call of the local authorities. They still remain servants of the Crown and chief constables have also to report to the Home Secretary at regular intervals.

The cost of running an efficient Police Service is considerable. Not only do police officers' salaries and premises have to be financed, but there are also vast armies of back-up staff to be employed to keep things running smoothly. Local authorities have to pay a proportion of the sums involved through local rates. Certain organisations (such as football clubs) that use the police also pay for the amenity. The remainder is made up from government grants. When licensed premises are permitted longer opening hours in 2005, the Home Office is considering a small levy on busy clubs and pubs, to cover some of the costs of anti-social behaviour outside their doors.

In the county forces the highest ranks operate from the county headquarters. Based here are the chief constable and his or her second-in-command, the deputy chief constable. They are assisted by a number of assistant chief constables, each being responsible for a specific area of operations. The area covered by the force is split up into divisions, with divisional police stations under the supervision of superintendents. These divisions are in turn made up of sub-divisions under the supervision of inspectors.

As in any other uniformed organisation, rank is shown by insignia worn on the jacket, and subordinates show their respect for the ranks above sergeant by addressing them as 'Sir' or 'Ma'am' (that's Ma'am as in charm, not Mam as in ham!). A constable carries a number on the epaulets (and a district letter in some areas); a sergeant has three stripes on the sleeve; an inspector wears two stars or 'pips' on the epaulets, a chief inspector three. Superintendents have a crown on their epaulets. Assistant chief constables and commanders carry insignia on their shoulder displaying crossed batons inside a wreath of bay leaves. Chief constables have a crown above the crossed batons and bay leaves, while the commissioner in the Metropolitan Police can be identified by his particular insignia of a crown above a single pip above the crossed batons and bay leaves.

Detective ranks parallel uniformed ranks and range from detective constable to detective chief superintendent. Because of the seriousness of some of the offences dealt with by the CID, the higher-ranking officers are more likely to be involved in operational work than their counterparts in uniform. The uniformed chief inspector, for example, spends most of the time in administration, while the CID counterpart frequently has to go out on serious crime inquiries. In murder investigations detective superintendents are in charge; the usual occasions when uniformed superintendents become involved in operational work are public order events, such as demonstrations or major incidents.

5

High Potential Development Scheme

FAST TRACK

HPDS (England, Wales and Northern Ireland)

The flexible fast-track police management scheme currently in operation in England, Wales and Northern Ireland is the High Potential Development Scheme (HPDS). It gives officers the opportunity of a structured streamlined career path through the Police Service.

First though you must pass the standard entry selection known as the National Assessment Process. If you successfully complete the probationary period and show the required potential, you will be steered rapidly into influential positions such as a responsible management role, or beyond to the strategic leadership level, all the way up to chief inspector, or even chief superintendent. The qualification can be compared to a Masters degree. As a leader you will have the opportunity to demonstrate your organisational abilities, people management skills and a strategic approach to problem solving.

APSG and APS (Scotland)

The Accelerated Promotion Scheme for Graduates (APSG), which was replaced by the HPDS in England, Wales and Northern Ireland, still exists at present in Scotland. If you are a graduate and interested in joining the scheme, you should contact the Scottish Police College for information (see Chapter 14 for the address). You must hold a degree at the time of application, or be in the final year of study (normally full-time) for a degree. The intensive scheme lasts between five and seven years, potentially leading you up the ladder to the rank of inspector or even chief inspector.

The benefits of this promotion scheme are also available to standard entrants who are graduates, and also non-graduates who have passed the Police Scotland Promotion Examination, and who show the desired promise and potential. Both groups can apply for the APSG belatedly.

Regardless of whether you are a graduate or not (or wishing to go on the scheme or not), you will have to undergo your chosen force's selection procedures first. After successfully completing this initial selection procedure, you can if you want elect to go forward to the next stage – the APSG selection process. The first stage is aptitude testing held in January of each year. If successful, you progress to a force selection board, where you will be interviewed and have to undergo individual or group exercises. Force selection takes place in February of each year. If you pass, you will be assessed at the Scottish Police College, usually in April, and candidates from all Scottish forces attend. Again this stage will probably consist of interviews, exercises and questionnaires. If you do well, a recommendation will be made to your force and you will be appointed as a constable under the scheme. Even if you are unsuccessful in the APSG selection procedure, you will most likely be offered an appointment under standard entry conditions, so you have nothing to lose.

All graduate entrants must serve a minimum of two years on the beat as a constable. This probationary period is vital, especially if APSG entrants are to reach managerial positions armed with a thorough understanding of police practices.

Not all graduates immediately opt to apply for the APSG – feeling they would be better suited to standard entry. Standard entrant trainees, however, can apply belatedly for the APSG, as long as it is within 12 months of joining, their degree is a 'recognisable' one (check this with the Scottish Police College), and they have not previously applied for the scheme.

All police officers, graduates or not, can apply for a place on an accelerated career path, once they have completed their probationary period and achieved good results in the promotion exam. The Service is constantly on the lookout for officers with potential and will provide them with the opportunity to rise quickly to the middle and senior ranks. Able officers can always find career satisfaction in the police, either through specialisation or promotion. Whether you are accepted on to a scheme or not, the Police Service offers a fulfilling career for people who value the challenges and rewards of public service.

The latest initiative from the Home Office to reduce crime and disorder is the 'Supercops' scheme, which is being introduced during 2004. Selected capable junior officers will be given specialist training and a lot of extra responsibility, including supervising teams of beat constables and police community support officers (PCSOs), or in the case of the CID of groups of civilian investigators. If this scheme is adopted across the country, there could be several thousand of these 'advanced skills' officers earning between £10,000 and £20,000 more than their colleagues.

6

Pay and pensions

PAY AND ALLOWANCES

Police officers' pay is controlled by the Secretary of State, with recommendations by the Police Negotiating Board. Pay is reviewed annually and pay awards are normally effective from 1 September. You will receive regular increments according to time spent in the rank. Competence-related threshold payments of around £1,000 may also be available to officers who have completed a certain number of years in the rank. The following general pay scales give you an idea what you can achieve at various ranks and stages in your career. Metropolitan Police officers and those from some other forces have higher basic pay and/or allowances to compensate for accommodation problems and travel difficulties and the high cost of living in their areas. Check the pay scales on the individual forces' Web sites.

Constables' pay

(Figures from 1 September 2003)

Pay point	£
On commencing service	19,227
On completion of initial training	21,462
2 years' service	22,707
3 years' service	23,298
4 years' service	24,096
5 years' service	24,852
6 years' service	25,650
7 years' service	26,382
8 years' service	27,039
9 years' service	27,903
10 years' service	28,914
11 years' service	29,589
12 years' service	30,186

Sergeants' pay

(Figures from 1 September 2003)

Pay point	£
On promotion	30,186
1st year in rank	31,221
2nd year in rank	32,268
3rd year in rank	32,958
4th year in rank	33,927

Inspectors' pay

(Figures from 1 September 2003)

Pay point	£
On promotion	38,679
1st year in rank	39,768
2nd year in rank	40,860
3rd year in rank	41,952

Chief Inspectors' pay

(Figures from 1 September 2003)

Pay point	£
On promotion	42,810
1st year in rank	43,671

Superintendents' pay

(Figures from 1 September 2003)

Pay point	£
1st year in rank	50,550
2nd year in rank	52,131
3rd year in rank	53,721
4th year in rank	56,190
5th year in rank	58,965

Chief Superintendents' pay

(Figures from 1 September 2003)

Pay point	£
1st year in rank	59,988
2nd year in rank	61,728
3rd year in rank	63,465

PENSIONS

As a police officer, you can join the Police Pension Scheme if you wish. If so, you will contribute 11 per cent of your pensionable pay. You may transfer contributions from a previous job, but there are some restrictions that you should investigate thoroughly first. Part-time officers pay contributions on a pro rata basis. It is generally recommended that all recruits should join this 'bucket' scheme for their own benefit (bearing in mind the recent publicity about some stock market-linked pensions). If you have any doubts, you should contact the Human Resources department or a Police Federation representative and discuss the situation.

Officers over the age of 50 (and youngsters below 50) can draw a pension of two-thirds pay, provided they have completed 30 years' service. Officers aged 50 who have completed 25 years' pensionable service will receive a pension that equates to half-pay. Your pension will be based on your highest pay during the last three years of your service. National Insurance contributions are paid at the lower contracted-out rate. At present, officers are allowed to commute part of their pension to a lump sum that is paid on retirement, depending on length of service and age. Pensions of retired officers over the age of 55 increase each year in line with the cost-of-living index.

7

Conditions of service

All conditions of service are constantly under review and therefore subject to change.

HOURS OF WORK

Full-time working

As a police officer you will have to work shifts, and each Service operates a different rota. The usual working week is 40 hours (five eight-hour shifts day or night), and if you are a constable, sergeant, inspector or chief inspector, you will be entitled to two rest days a week and eight public holidays per year. Should you be asked to work on these days (which you occasionally will be), leave or compensation in lieu will be granted.

Part-time working

It may be possible for you to work part-time or to job-share, in which case the same pay, terms and conditions generally apply, albeit on a pro rata basis. While on probation, however, you are obliged to work an average of at least 24 hours a week and your initial training must be completed on a full-time basis. You will also have to work shifts and night duties.

Overtime

It is the nature of the job that you may occasionally be called in to the station to deal with an emergency, so you should be prepared for some disruption to your personal life. If you are required to work on one of your rest days, overtime is paid in accordance with some very strict rules. Where less than five days' notice has been given to you, the hours that you work will be paid at the 'double time' rate. Where less than 15 days' notice has been given, you will be paid at 'time and a half'. And where more than 15 days' notice is given, you will receive another rest day in lieu. If you are a part-time officer, you will be paid at the 'plain time' rate for your extra hours worked, unless they exceed 40 hours a week.

Where less than eight days' notice is received to work a public holiday, you will get 'double time' pay and a day off. Where more than eight days' notice is given, just 'double time' is payable. Alternatively, you can choose to have time off in lieu of payment.

Quite often, overtime is not pre-planned – you may still be interviewing a prisoner or completing vital paperwork at the end of your shift. The first 30 minutes of this 'casual overtime' will be unpaid, unless more than four of them have been worked during a week.

LEAVE

Annual leave

For the first five years of your service, including your two-year probationary period, you can take 21 days annual leave per year, on top of public holidays. This will increase as you proceed through the Service. For example, you will be entitled to 29 days after 20 years' service. Part-time officers will get the same amount of leave on a pro rata basis.

Maternity and adoption leave

You will be entitled to maximum maternity leave of six months before and nine months after the birth. You have the right to return to work afterwards – it may then be possible to do part-time or job-share. Three months' paid maternity leave is given, provided you have served continuously for a year or more by the start of the 11th week before the birth and are still pregnant, or have given birth 15 weeks before the expected birth date. The father, partner or nominated carer is also entitled to five days' paid maternity support leave. If you are adopting a child, you will be given five days' paid leave.

Sick leave

Should you be unfortunate enough to be off-duty because of illness or injury, you will receive full pay for six months in any one-year period, and then half pay for six months.

ACCOMMODATION

Some constabularies still have section houses for single officers and a limited number of police houses. You can check the monthly cost of section rooms with the recruitment officer or Human Resources department. You will have to weigh up the section house costs versus private rental (probably sharing with friends or other colleagues), and of course living at home with your parents is usually very cheap! Everyone's circumstances are different, of course. You may be a mature entrant and already own your own home. Whatever the situation, your accommodation requires formal approval. Rent/housing allowance used to be an accepted benefit of the job, but it was abolished for new recruits and frozen for serving officers in 1994. There are transitional allowances in place and increases in pay and other allowances to compensate, but the situation varies from area to area, so you will need to specifically ask your force about it.

You must not expect to be stationed near to your home (though you can always ask). In the larger constabularies, you could be posted a considerable distance away, so a for certain period of time you should be prepared to travel long distances, or relocate. If you are in police accommodation, the cost of removal may be borne by the local Police Authority and an allowance paid in respect of expenditure incidental to the move. But this is another thing you need to check out with the individual force concerned.

Hotspots

In the last few years the cost of housing in certain hotspots throughout the country has literally gone through the roof. Originating in London, it has spread to many other parts of the UK, and is now causing tremendous problems for housing essential workers. This of course affects many young police officers, as they have been effectively priced out of the market. There are various initiatives in hand to try and provide low-cost housing in expensive areas, but it is a serious problem for many forces and Police Authorities.

CODE OF CONDUCT

You must at all times avoid behaviour likely to discredit the Police Service or interfere with the impartial discharge of your duties, such as the following:

- Neither you nor your partner can have business interests that might jeopardise your position as a police officer.

- You should not take an active part in politics.

- Failure to discharge debts must be reported.

Misconduct

During your probationary period, if you misbehave or are not fit to perform your duties effectively, you will be dismissed. One month's notice or a month's pay in lieu will be given, plus a refund of any pension contributions. If you wish to resign, you must give one month's notice in writing, unless the Police Authority accepts a shorter period.

Unfitness

The Home Office is currently developing an occupational health programme to reduce injuries and ill health in police staff and to help those that have been ill to return to work and full performance. You are expected to maintain an acceptable level of fitness during your service. Repeated failure to pass fitness tests may lead to your discharge.

8

Equality and diversity

RACE, GENDER AND CONFUSION

Diversity

In recent years there has been considerable debate on the issue of race relations and the police. The Police Service has been forced to analyse in minute detail its attitude towards minorities and purge any racial discrimination found within its ranks, so that all members of society can be confident they will be treated with fairness, consistency and dignity. It is also concentrating on becoming much more representative of its mixed communities. The Scarman Report of 1982 states that 'a police force which fails to reflect the ethnic diversity of our society will never succeed in securing the full support of all its sections', and the report of the Stephen Lawrence Inquiry mirrors that view. These recommendations have been given legal force with the Race Relations (Amendment) Act 2000, which ensures race equality in the delivery of public services. The Government has put in place a programme right across the public sector. As part of this, race equality employment targets are set for the Civil Service as a whole.

Below are examples of some of the latest initiatives, definitions and offences that have to be absorbed by the newly fledged police officer. The glut of racial schemes may appear 'politically correct' and somewhat 'over the top', but they reinforce essential standards of decency in our multicultural society. It is just a matter of common sense. If you value people, you tend to get a positive response from them, as opposed to resentment. The advice was less complex three decades ago when I joined the police, and I was simply told to 'treat everyone as you would treat members of your own family' – that is, not necessarily all the same, but according to circumstance and always with a bit of respect!

Racial offences

There has been a steep rise in recorded racial incidents over the last 20 years. 'Racial offence' is defined by the Association of Chief Police Officers (ACPO) as:

> any incident in which it appears to the reporting or investigating officer that the complaint involves an element of racial motivation; or any incident which includes an allegation of racial motivation made by any person.

This can include major and minor assaults, threats and abuse, or criminal damage to property belonging to members of a specific group, defined by their colour, ethnic origin or nationality. The interpretation of the above means that colour could indicate black or white; ethnic origin – Indian or Gypsy, etc; and nationality – Albanian, Belgian, and so on. ACPO further states that 'there should be a presumption towards prosecution in all racially motivated incidents...' and if it is proved that racial hostility or motivation lies behind the crime in question, the offence may become a racially aggravated one, leading to the possibility of a much stiffer punishment.

A number of new offences of racially aggravated assaults have been created: 'racially aggravated malicious wounding or racially aggravated grievous bodily harm'; 'racially aggravated actual bodily harm'; and 'racially aggravated common assault'. Offences such as murder, manslaughter or grievous bodily harm with intent already carry maximum sentences of life imprisonment. However, evidence of racial hostility can be viewed as an aggravating factor meriting an increased sentence. A new offence of 'racially aggravated criminal damage' is now in use, which might include abusive graffiti, for example, and new racially aggravated public order offences have been brought in. Offences of racially aggravated harassment have been created and the Police and Criminal Evidence Act 1984 (PACE) has been amended to include a power of arrest for such crimes.

Racism in the police

Police officers are still reeling from the accusation of 'institutional racism'. Great effort has since been expended on restoring the reputation of the police as a fair and just organisation. There would not be enough room in this section to describe all the legislation and reports, training initiatives, guidelines and articles that have been produced on this subject, but it is an indication of just how seriously the Police Service has taken the problem over the last few years.

Just one proactive example is a guide called *'The Power of Language'* that has recently been circulated by Greater Manchester Police. The aim is to protect staff from making unintentional mistakes in the terminology they use, specifically setting out what language is acceptable and what is not. Language relating to race, gender, religion, disability, and sexual orientation is covered. It has been produced because of a general lack of awareness as to what words could be deemed offensive and why.

The frank statement on the Federation Web site by the Chairman of the Police Federation of England and Wales, Jan Berry, indicates the strength of feeling within the Police Service about the current state of affairs. She was reacting to a critical 'fly on the wall' television documentary in which racist language was used at a police training college. In defence of all the staff she represents, she makes it clear that 'the vast majority of police officers are not racist and do not condone racism'. She says:

> As individuals they have played a key role in the determined efforts that have been made over many years to stamp out racism; these efforts must and will continue. Some new recruits will join the police with a range of views that are at best thoughtless and at worst totally unacceptable. The Police Service must learn from this. It must review its procedures for recruitment to enable it to better identify unsuitable officers at a far earlier stage and then take any necessary action. The Service must also ensure that police officers feel able to challenge and report inappropriate behaviour. With growing numbers of recruits joining the Service and police numbers at an all time high it is vital that policing is seen to be an attractive career for everyone regardless of gender, religion, culture, disability or ethnicity.

Recruitment campaign

Currently, the numbers of ethnic minority and female officers in the Police Service do not reflect the population. The Government has created the 'Dismantling Barriers Initiative', which includes a national target of 7 per cent by 2009 for the employment of officers, special constables and support staff from minority ethnic communities. Furthermore, the national police recruitment campaign titled 'Could You?' aims to redress the balance and is generating a lot of interest with its comprehensive Web site. As a result, individual police forces around the country have been inundated with enquiries – a large proportion of them from women, and an encouraging number from ethnic minorities.

Women currently account for 17 per cent of the total number of established officers, and 27 per cent of recruits. However, since females form 44 per cent of the 'economically active population', the police need to attract a larger number. Magazine articles have been used to promote the idea of a career in the Police Service as an exciting and worthwhile job. Steps have also been taken to make the Service more female-friendly, such as modifying the 'upper body dynamic strength' element of the fitness test, and introducing the High Potential Development Scheme, a flexible career development programme that is particularly attractive to women.

Positive action

The Metropolitan Police Service (MPS) has formed the Positive Action Central Team (PACT), with the intention of providing London with a fully representative body. It aims to provide positive support to people interested in joining the police, particularly those from under-represented communities. PACT targets ethnic groups who may be unaware of the possibility of a police career, perhaps due to social discrimination or peer pressure. Female applicants are also actively encouraged to apply for a job in the police. Schools, youth clubs, businesses and religious groups are all supplied with career information and advice, including details of the two-day Metropolitan Police selection procedure.

The Metropolitan Police deny it is an example of 'positive discrimination'. Applicants do not receive an unfair advantage – everyone has to pass the same minimum entry requirements and subsequently progress on merit alone. It is not illegal or unfair to raise awareness among particular groups of potential applicants prior to selection. The aim is to allow candidates from minority ethnic groups to compete with others on equal terms. The Race Relations Act in any event does not permit reverse discrimination or affirmative action.

Case Study

Nina (PC – age 27 – three years' service – community liaison)

It was difficult for me to become a police officer because I was raised in a very strict Asian household, and it caused a lot of problems for my family in the beginning. One of my girlfriends told me she was thinking about joining the police. She had been sent two application packs by mistake and said I should apply as well. I thought it was an opportunity to live my own life a bit. So I filled out the forms and my friend took them with her and explained my situation to the recruitment office. Weeks later a female officer in plain clothes called on me at home when my father was away and we talked everything over. As a result she returned the next evening with a male officer – Indian like us. While he spoke to my father, she spoke to my mother. The result of all this discussion was that both my parents said they would support me, after receiving assurances from the police that my religion and customs would be respected. This proved to be true right from the start, even though I felt some people were bending over backwards to include me in everything, when I just wanted to be part of the team without any fuss.

It all settled down in time and now, three amazing years later, my friend and I feel like old timers. I am a community liaison officer and love what I do. I look wiry but I am actually quite tough, so some of the things I hear do not bother me. I just hope that I can build a bridge between the local people and the police. I still live at home and switch off as soon as I change out of the uniform. I know that my parents are privately proud of what I have achieved and my father is much more accepting of the situation.

GENDER AGENDA

In response to particular problems affecting women police officers, the Gender Agenda was launched in 2001. Among other things, it promotes the idea that women officers should be actively recruited and encouraged in their career development, with an even gender balance throughout all ranks and specialist units. Their skills should be valued and opinions heeded in important policy decision-making, and their hopes for a successful work/home-life balance encouraged. It recommends that training courses be set up on a more family-friendly basis with regard to timing and location.

Career development

Female officers are now to be found in the top ranks of the Police Service, having fought their way up the highly competitive promotion ladder. The new High Potential Development Scheme was introduced in 2002 and applies to England, Wales and Northern Ireland. It particularly appeals to women officers. This scheme is more flexible than its predecessor, the Accelerated Promotion Scheme (still in operation in Scotland), providing an individually planned, competence-based career development programme, where officers are in control of their own progress. There are more opportunities to join, take a break from the scheme, and study during work time.

DISABILITY

There are over 8½ million people who are disabled in the UK, some of them police employees – either civilian staff or serving officers who have become disabled through injuries caused while on duty. At the end of 2004, the Disability Discrimination Act will come into force and cover operational police officers for the first time. Police Services are waiting for an update regarding future law, and practical guidance on how to make reasonable adjustments; how this affects their operational capability; and how they can produce clear policies for treating staff fairly.

In partnership with the Employers' Forum on Disability, the Association of Chief Police Officers (ACPO) has set up the Police Disability Network to help the police employ and look after the interests of disabled people. There are more than 40 members, including the National Crime Squad and the Metropolitan Police. Many forces have set up initiatives to help the disabled, ranging from easier-accessed police station lobbies to text messaging for hearing- and speech-impaired people. The Home Office has commissioned research into the occupational health and physical fitness standards for applicants, to try and ensure that they are non-discriminatory and fair. If you need more detailed information, you should contact your chosen force and enquire about their disability policy.

9

Police departments

SPOILT FOR CHOICE

There are so many departments within the Police Service, that if you are looking for a change of emphasis in your career, you really will be spoilt for choice.

There are many occasions when the senior officer in charge of a major incident has to draw on the expertise of various specialist units to help with the police operation – units such as CID, traffic, mounted police, dog handlers or air support, to name just a few.

Criminal Investigation Department

To the uninitiated, working in the Criminal Investigation Department (CID) suggests an action-packed lifestyle, as portrayed on television or film. The true picture is that of a job with some very interesting moments, but which is usually more concerned with painstaking routine.

Much of detectives' work at the police station is concerned with the investigation of serious crimes (burglaries, robberies, fraud, sexual offences, serious assaults and murders). They also assist uniformed officers in investigating less serious crimes. Policing has shifted over the last few years from the reactive investigation (after the event) towards the proactive targeting of all offenders, in other words intelligence-led policing. However, because of time constraints, there is often little time for such preventive action, and CID officers currently still respond mainly to crimes that have already been committed. On occasions some of these cannot always be given the full attention they deserve – each case taking such a long time to process with all the attendant paperwork. Reported crimes have to be continually prioritised, which is upsetting for victims.

Within the CID there are certain specialist departments that deal with the prevention and detection of large-scale organised crime. However, before officers can be considered for a job in any of these, they must have proven experience in the more routine aspects of detective work.

CID officers do not work the regular three-shift system like their uniformed colleagues. The hours are frequently long and irregular, with a good deal of evening and some night and weekend work. If they get involved in a murder inquiry, for example, they may spend several weeks or months on a minimum of sleep and see very little of their home and family. Officers must be prepared to collect and sift information by means of slow, painstaking and often frustrating inquiries. A good memory, an eye for detail and the ability to assess people's characters accurately are all particularly useful for this work.

Large numbers of police constables apply to join the CID but few are selected. Every force has its own department, but only one in eight of all police officers belong to it and a proportion of these are in the specialist branches, so vacancies are few. A preliminary step to transferring may well be to go on temporary attachment to a particular squad. If officers show obvious talent for this type of work, they may then be encouraged by their senior officer, who will recommend them for consideration by an interview board. The rank and pay structure is similar to that of the uniformed police.

Case Study

Ralph (DC – age 45 – 19 years' service – inner-city station)

My father was in the police force and he wanted me to join too, but I was young and rebellious, so I went into the army instead. It was a good job and I enjoyed it, but once I got married, I wanted a more settled home life, so I applied to the police. I didn't tell my Dad until I was accepted, in case I failed and embarrassed myself. He didn't say much at the time, but years afterwards, he told me how pleased he had been about my decision, although he had worried that I might find it very frustrating at times because I wouldn't necessarily get results straight away, like in the army. The military training helped me right from the start. I was always in the thick of the action. My only problem was understanding all the legal complexities of the job – I'm definitely going to encourage my kids to become lawyers!

I found being a uniformed constable a bit tame and applied for attachment to crime squads. After that it was a natural progression to the CID, where I have remained ever since. It's incredibly varied and yes, it is frustrating if you can't get convictions, but you learn to put it to one side. I can handle all the actions of the investigation, the arrest, interview, etc, and even the crazy paperwork. It was giving evidence at court that used to be a problem. I'm definitely not a public speaker, so standing up and being the focus of attention was not my cup of tea. Also, and this is unlike me, I used to get stupidly nervous waiting in the court corridor, not of course that you would have noticed it. The civilian witnesses waiting with me would also be worried and it was my job to calm them down and reassure them it would be all right, while pretending to be relaxed myself. After several court cases though, it just becomes automatic. In court you just have to stick religiously to the truth, whole truth, etc, and you can always refer to your notebook in court if you can't remember every single detail about incidents that happened many months ago (who can?). My own daughter has just chipped in to say that she is thinking about joining the police, so I'd better tell her to go ahead, so she can, like me, do the complete opposite, and maybe become a lawyer after all!

Serious Organised Crime Agency

A new body known as the Serious Organised Crime Agency (SOCA) will begin work in 2006, merging the National Crime Squad, National Criminal Intelligence Service, parts of the Immigration Service and Customs and Excise. This British 'FBI' will target professional criminals involved in drug, gun and people smuggling, as well as money laundering and hi-tech crime.

The Agency will be supported by specialist prosecutors and accountants.

National Crime Squad

The National Crime Squad was founded in 1998 to combat the threat of organised crime and replaced the six separate Regional Crime Squads with a nationally coordinated force. It has close links to the Scottish Crime Squad, and can draw on the support of other law enforcement, security and intelligence agencies, such as Customs and Excise and the National Criminal Intelligence Service. A Director General heads the squad, which operates from its headquarters in London.

A few thousand officers are seconded from police forces in England and Wales, aided by support staff employed by the National Crime Squad Service Authority. Operations include undercover work, physical or technical surveillance, witness protection and financial investigation. The National Crime Squad targets criminal organisations responsible for serious and organised crime nationally and internationally. Crimes range from drug trafficking to money laundering, contract killing, kidnapping, illegal arms deals, counterfeit currency, and extortion. Drug investigations account for around three-quarters of all cases. Operations can take months, even years, before an arrest can be made.

National Criminal Intelligence Service

The National Criminal Intelligence Service (NCIS) produces reports on intelligence gleaned from police, Customs and Excise, Government agencies and other bodies at home and overseas. It shares sensitive information about what is known collectively about the various threats posed by serious and organised criminals, who trade in drugs, people and illicit goods. It also collects intelligence on hi-tech crime, fraud, money laundering, firearms, sex offenders and online abuse of children, and many other related crimes.

Force Intelligence Department

Some local forces have their own intelligence departments (which go under various names). They target active criminals by developing intelligence on the most serious offenders, and acting as the central point for internal and external enquiries, including the 'Crimestoppers' scheme. Analytical units provide strategic assessments based on trends – this is known as intelligence-led policing. They also liaise with national and international law enforcement agencies, as well as local community organisations and businesses. They have to comply with the Data Protection Act, which governs how police collect, analyse and disseminate information on suspected offenders.

Drugs Squad

Most forces have squads to deal with serious drug offences. Their work involves the surveillance of local drug dealers and raids on suspects' premises. The teams frequently liaise with the National Crime Squad where large-scale drug trafficking is involved. The surge in drug-related crime over the past few decades has been a major cause for concern for every force in the country.

The Government recently launched a national drug strategy called 'Tackling Drugs to Build a Better Britain'. Local forces will be working with representatives from different agencies, such as the council, health authority, education department, probation service and local prisons, in the areas of drug prevention, treatment and enforcement.

Fraud Squad

This department is known by different names across the country (Commercial Branch, for example). A number of forces have specialist officers dealing with this type of crime. The definition of fraud is getting money or goods illegally from people or businesses by deception. The specialist Fraud Squad in London was set up in 1946 and run jointly by the Metropolitan Police and the City of London Police. There is also the Serious Fraud Office, a Government department specially set up to investigate and prosecute large-scale fraud. Fraud affects every one of us. It affects both the public and private sectors, and costs around £12 billion a year. Sound fraud prevention measures are essential.

Specialist Operations

Constabularies across the country have their own specialist departments, which are known under different titles, but in one form or another contain the same ingredients. Specialist Operations (SO) is part of the Metropolitan Police's Specialist Crime Directorate. The Directorate consists of three groups – Forensic Services, Intelligence and Serious Crime Group, and the Business Services Group. Some of these specialist units working across London also fulfil a national role. SO deals mainly with matters relating to intelligence, security, the protection of politicians, embassies and royalty, and the investigation of certain categories of serious crimes, including racial and violent crime, and of course terrorism. Some of the units involved in the Met include the Anti-Terrorist Branch, the National Identification Service, Special Branch, the Royal and Diplomatic Branch and Firearms Branch.

Case Study

Dawn (Scene of Crime Officer – age 31 – 7 years' service)

When I left university with a science degree, I thought about joining the police, but I had family commitments at the time, caring for my mother who had cancer, and I knew I would not be able to manage the shift pattern, particularly nights. I put my career plans on hold for a few years until she died. I had a part-time job in my local hospital's pathology department and over the years developed a keen interest in forensic science. I suppose I could have carried on working in the laboratory, but I felt I wanted to be at the 'sharp end', so I chose to apply to be a SOCO – and it was the best decision I could have made.

Forensic evidence is becoming more and more important in court cases, and I can play a vital part in finding fingerprints or blood samples that may secure the identification of a suspect. The role is developing all the time as new methods are constantly being introduced, so life is never dull. Most of the time I am out of the office and my own boss, but still part of the team. I don't suppose I will ever get used to a murder scene – it still shakes me up – but helping the victims of crime, by securing exhibits to prove the case against the accused, makes the job worthwhile.

Anti-Terrorist Branch

The Anti-Terrorist Branch was formed in the 1970s. Staffed by experienced detectives, surveillance officers and forensic scene examiners, it deals with politically motivated crimes, economic terrorism, extortion and animal rights extremism. The Counter-Terrorist Search Wing advises and offers training in protective security against terrorism.

Special Branch

Special Branch was started by the Metropolitan Police in 1883 to deal specifically with the threat of the Irish Fenians who were causing explosions in the city. It subsequently expanded its activities to encompass any foreign national who might possibly be a threat to the United Kingdom or to British subjects. (Karl Marx and Lenin for instance came under surveillance while they were studying here.) During the two world wars, Special Branch worked with M15 keeping an eye on possible spies.

Today it gathers and analyses intelligence on extremist political and terrorist activity, and passes the information on to law enforcement agencies at local, national and international levels. The value of intelligence cannot be overstated. Special Branch also provides armed personal protection for politicians, foreign VIPs and others at threat from terrorists or extremism. It investigates firearms or explosives offences that may be connected to national security. The ports are kept under observation to detect terrorist or criminal suspects travelling in or out of the country. It also assists other Government agencies to counter threats to the security of the United Kingdom from public disorder, espionage by foreign powers, subversion of the democratic process, terrorism by international groups and sabotage of the country's infrastructure.

In some forces that have their own Special Branch, officers join the department via the CID and have to prove themselves there before they can apply to transfer. In the Metropolitan Police, its members are generally recruited from the uniformed branch direct. Knowledge of foreign languages can be a great advantage.

Royal and Diplomatic Branch

These armed officers protect the Sovereign and members of the Royal Family both at their UK residences and abroad, as well as politicians, visiting foreign royal families, heads of state, diplomats and their embassies in the UK. They are also responsible for escorting high-risk prisoners, accompanying particularly valuable loads, and providing security at New Scotland Yard. All officers are expert drivers and are trained in the use of different types of firearms and self-protection methods.

A division specifically looks after the Houses of Parliament. The police safeguard the buildings, prevent disorder and unauthorised access, and investigate any reported crime. Officers accompany VIPs during visits and are present in the public galleries. Terrorism is a constant threat in such a high profile location, so they are constantly alert.

Firearms Branch

The use of dangerous weapons is a very real threat nowadays. Each force has a specialist team trained to deal with a variety of armed situations. The training is extremely thorough, and the qualities of calmness and quick thinking are valued along with expert marksmanship. Some forces have also set up special firearms enquiries teams that handle enquiries relating to the licensing and legal possession of shotguns or firearms.

The Forensic Science Service is soon to launch its National Firearms Forensic Intelligence Database. The aim is to improve the speed and quality of police intelligence sharing on firearms used in crime and to bring more criminals to justice. Further initiatives on gun crime have recently included a national firearms amnesty, and a 5-year minimum sentence for illegal possession of prohibited firearms (Criminal Justice Act). The Anti-Social Behaviour Act bans easily converted air guns, the carrying of air guns and replicas in public, increases the minimum age of ownership of air weapons to 17, and targets gun crime with intelligence-led operations such as Operation Trident.

OTHER DEPARTMENTS

Other specialist units include (among many others) Traffic, Air Support, Public Order, Mounted Branch, River Police and the Underwater Search Unit, and Dog Handlers.

Traffic Department

Most people think of the traffic 'cop' as someone concerned mainly with speeding motorists, but the job is far more involved.

Officers who join the Traffic Department will quickly discover that they are concerned with every aspect of safety on the road, although their priority is to reduce accidents. They will also be responsible for keeping the ever-increasing flow of vehicles moving through the towns, and dealing with motorway pile-ups. Cars and lorries on the road will have to be checked to see if they conform to the safety requirements laid down by law, including hazardous chemical transporters. Abnormal loads have to be escorted from one end of the country to the other, and roadworks monitored. Traffic officers may one moment stop a motorist for dangerous driving, and the next come to the aid of a badly injured road accident victim. Once they have dealt with the aftermath of several car crashes, they may well have a different 'take' on the importance of speed restrictions!

Drivers of traffic cars (not to be confused with drivers of patrol cars, which belong to the police station) and motorcycles operate independently out of special centralised traffic garages. From there they go out on patrol and are called to incidents requiring a police presence (such as accidents, roadblocks, major hold-ups and so on). They will have been highly trained at one of the regional driving schools to enable them to drive at speed but in safety, and also have taken courses in the specialist knowledge required, including vehicle regulations governing height, weight, speed and so on. Road accidents will have to be dealt with efficiently and traffic chaos kept to a minimum when damaged vehicles are blocking the road. Measurements and diagrams of crash scenes have to be carefully produced for use as evidence in court, in cases of careless or dangerous driving. Officers will also become familiar with the procedure for breathalysing and arresting drink drivers.

Though traffic specialists, they are still police officers and will naturally get involved in all sorts of non-traffic incidents. They could have suspicions about a particular vehicle and want to question the occupants, with unpredictable results if the passengers are wanted criminals.

Air Support Unit

The first known use of air operations was in 1921, when the Metropolitan Police used an airship to monitor traffic on Derby Day. There are now many forces operating with full-time helicopter and aircraft support. On-board technology includes thermal imaging cameras, which 'see in the dark' by following heat sources. Pictures are relayed to ground commanders, giving them valuable crime management information. The unit comprises both police observers and civilian pilots. With a bird's eye view of the search area, the versatility and speed of air support make it a valuable asset in, for example, finding missing persons, evacuating casualties and moving essential personnel to the heart of any operation.

Public Order Unit

The police have to be well prepared for public disorder problems, whether during strikes, protest marches, or fights between football supporters. The Public Order Training Centre (POTC) trains London officers in the skills needed to deal with a wide range of public order problems, and it is also a training provider for other forces. Some Police Services, of course, have their own training provision. Training facilities include film sets of streets with fake buildings, where full-scale riots can be simulated, and officers learn how to cope with all sorts of missile attacks, including petrol bombs. Mounted officers also take an active part. This branch of the police is known by various names throughout the Constabularies.

Mounted Police

Not every force has a mounted branch and those that do generally have a long waiting list of would-be applicants. Four out of five applicants are rejected. The history of the Mounted Branch is long, honourable and distinguished, and in the past many recruits were drawn from cavalry regiments. Nowadays, good equestrian skills are not necessarily required, but since a quarter of the selection marks are based on a riding assessment, plus a fitness test and interview, some riding experience would logically be an advantage.

Probationers receive expert training in riding and correct stable management at one of the specialist training centres, with regular refresher courses every year. They ride and care for a different horse every month, until eventually they get their own mount. The training procedure involves using tapes of loud noises, bangs, crashes, traffic noise, shouting and screaming to acclimatise the horse. Mounted officers are taught the lateral movement into crowds, which is the safest and most effective method of crowd control for horse and public.

Mounted police provide a high visibility police presence, which is a deterrent against hooliganism, street robbery, vandalism, theft from motor vehicles and burglary. Patrolling in parks and on common land deters both anti-social or indecent behaviour and criminal damage.

Horses can be invaluable for crowd control during potentially violent confrontations or crush situations at demonstrations and sporting events. A mounted officer can be as effective as a dozen officers on foot. There is something rather formidable about a mounted officer and the rioter on foot generally respects this. In rural areas, such as parts of Scotland, horses are also useful during searches of wide areas of moorland. In London, the Metropolitan Police horses are ridden around the streets on regular patrol, and still form part of most ceremonial occasions. Mounted Branch officers often act as the Sovereign's escort, and in the last few years have led both Princess Diana's and the Queen Mother's funeral processions.

Mounted officers are responsible for the care of their horses before and after taking them out, and are expected to pass an examination in stable management and veterinary care as well as horsemanship. They usually have to groom their own horses, taking them for shoeing and being responsible for their equipment, although they may have some assistance from civilian grooms.

They are expected to stay within the branch for a number of years and since units are generally quite small, opportunities for promotion are necessarily limited. Of course, they are first and foremost police officers, so they must demonstrate competence at normal duties during the first two probation years if they want to be considered.

River Police

Some forces with large rivers or coastal waters within their boundaries need special contingents to police them.

The number of vacancies for such specialised work naturally varies according to the amount of waterways to be policed, so those who are attracted to a career afloat should choose the force they apply to with this in mind. Again, competition is keen and officers cannot go into the waterborne division without the initial two-year period on foot patrol. Swimming ability and competence in the handling of boats (such as sailing experience) are obvious assets.

River police in patrol boats and motor launches deal with thefts from ships, warehouses and houseboats, help craft in difficulties, and examine wharves, dock entrances, riverside premises and landing places. They also rescue people (or salvage bodies) from the water; secure drifting boats, pick up derelict timber and the like, which can cause navigation hazards; and monitor water pollution (such as oil spillages). They also work closely with Customs and Excise to prevent smuggling, and can be called upon to help in the pursuit of those wanted by the uniformed branch or the CID.

Underwater Search Unit

There are many forces with underwater search units (sometimes known by other names) manned by highly trained divers. They need to be extremely fit to be considered for a posting to one of these teams, as they may well be called out in the depths of winter to search under half-frozen ponds or other stretches of water for missing people, stolen property or suspected murder weapons. Units are usually very small and opportunities are limited.

Dog Handlers

Police dogs have been used regularly since the end of the Second World War and they have proved invaluable for finding missing persons and property and for catching criminals.

Dog handlers must be prepared for a long-term commitment, since dog and handler become an inseparable team. The dog may well be 'puppy walked' until it is old enough to begin work. Handler and dog will certainly train together and it will usually be taught to answer only to the handler's commands. The dog will live with and become part of the family, and on retirement (at about nine years old), it will generally stay on and become a pet.

Candidates cannot apply to work in the dog section until they have first proved that they are good police officers by successfully completing their statutory two years on shift work. Then they may be given a trial course with a dog trained to accept commands from more than one person.

A genuine love of animals and infinite patience are needed, and handlers must be fit enough to keep up with their dogs on the various exercises involved. Then they may be placed on a waiting list until a vacancy occurs. Police dogs and their handlers are very highly trained and attend constant refresher courses throughout their active service. The dogs must learn obedience, so that they are always under complete control, even in the heat of a chase or when confronted with strange noises (such as gunshots).

They must be taught nose-work – the tracking of people or objects without being distracted by other more attractive scents (such as food or cats), and man work – the pursuit and capture of a suspect by gripping but not biting until the handler arrives. In addition, some dogs are taught how to sniff out drugs and explosives. Officers are not only taught how to give clear commands, but also how to care for their dogs and keep them in the peak of condition necessary for such active work.

Alsatians are widely used in British police forces. Other breeds used are Labradors (particularly good as 'sniffer' dogs), Weimaraners, Dobermans and Rottweilers. Dogs and handlers have to be available at all times and so they work one of the three shifts, either on foot, in vans, or on call at the station. Many police dogs are now specially bred in police kennels so that forces can keep up a constant supply of the right sort of animal (both in breed and temperament), although a certain number are still bought in or given by the public, while young enough to be trained properly.

Recently there was a much-publicised pilot project where police took sniffer dogs unannounced into schools to do a spot check on drugs in classrooms and lockers, as part of a drug prevention and education initiative. They also took in a scanner called an ion track tester, originally designed to detect explosives at airports. Needless to say, the Department of Education and civil liberties groups were not amused! The force had bought the scanner using a grant from the Government's 'Community against Drugs Fund'.

Mobile Police Support Unit

Experienced officers may apply to serve for a limited period in the Mobile Police Support Units of their force. These are highly flexible units that can be brought in at short notice to assist local officers, should additional manpower be needed for specific purposes – to police football matches and demonstrations, or to combat a particularly high incidence of burglaries, shoplifting offences or robberies by organised gangs. They are also used in large-scale searches for missing persons, murder weapons, etc, and play a prominent part in sieges and similar incidents.

These units have different titles and functions across the forces. Some specialist support units offer tactical support in specific areas of expertise. They can be called in to conduct house-to-house enquiries, forced entry and fingertip searches (for example, the Tactical Aid Group). They also work in conjunction with other forces and agencies where offenders cross boundaries.

Child Protection Team

These teams investigate allegations or suspicions of child abuse. They work with the relevant Social Services departments and representatives of other caring agencies. Child abuse can relate to any situation where a child does not receive the proper standard of care expected from a reasonable parent. This of course includes sexual abuse, physical neglect or emotional abuse. Officers must be sympathetic yet unemotional, as some of the cases can be distressing.

Youth and Community Unit

Seventy-five per cent of police time is spent dealing with juvenile crime, and most police forces have a special system for dealing with these young people (a juvenile is defined as someone who has not yet reached the age of 17). The police support the many schemes on offer nowadays, seeking to divert potential young offenders from their wicked ways. If nothing was done, communities would be swamped by a youth crime culture, usually fuelled by drink and drugs, which undermine all police efforts. Education and employment are two important factors in the equation, and cooperation between police, schools, drug clinics, social services and local employers is encouraged. Teaching responsible citizenship, together with appropriate and speedy punishment (while the offence is fresh in the mind) seems to be the way forward. The victims now have a chance to confront their young attackers, to help them see the error of their ways. The offender's family is also involved and encouraged to help and/or discipline their youngster as the case may be. Young offenders are monitored through their formative years and provided with support and training opportunities.

Youth affairs officers work in the schools and set up bullying surgeries, helping children avoid confrontational situations. They also help with Duke of Edinburgh Schemes and organise life skills projects. Forces around the country operate many initiatives targeting youth crime, and communities are invited to participate.

Although the bulk of youngsters grow out of their offending behaviour, there is always a small hardcore that commit a disproportionate amount of crime, and fail to respond to community service orders. Just one hooligan can create havoc in a community, and will probably only respond to a custodial sentence.

Community Involvement

Some forces have units that concern themselves with community partnerships and advise on current good practice. Their aim is to provide a strategic response and they are driven by the need to ensure value for money, so that more funds are directed to operational policing. Such units are sometimes known by a different name in Constabularies around the country.

Staff, who may be civilians, could be involved in producing anything from a simple advisory video to an integrated campaign involving operational officers, the media, the Web, Neighbourhood Watch and local authorities. The finished product is then used as a means to reduce demand on police. Finance and resources are then provided to fund local solutions to locally identified problems. Policy frameworks are produced to guide commanding officers, ensuring a corporate approach to national objectives.

Community safety units recognise the special support needed by victims of hate crimes (homophobic or racial), rape and domestic violence. Uniformed officers may be assigned a victim and act as his or her point of contact for the duration of the case, so a calm compassionate personality is required. Often staff liaise closely with local Victim Support units.

10

Civilian support services

CIVILIAN CAREER OPPORTUNITIES

You may not think you could be a police officer, but perhaps there is a career in the Service for you as a support specialist.

Police officers in the front line of crime fighting would not be able to function without the help of the many thousands of specialist support staff employed around the country. Some departments are completely civilian and others consist of a mixture of police officers and civilian staff. Their activities are diverse, and include occupations such as scenes of crime officers, human resources, custody officers, force intelligence, IT support, cleaners, lawyers, public relations, accountants, station reception officers, caterers, and clerical staff.

Descriptions of just a handful of them are listed in this chapter. The Service provides a challenging environment for career development, with ample scope for training and promotion. Support staff application forms are available when vacancies arise for positions. These are widely advertised in the press and Job Centres, and also on police force Web sites. After the initial paper sift of forms, you will be contacted to attend for interview.

Station Reception Officers

Station reception officers are the initial points of contact for anyone visiting a police station to report a crime or lost property, to produce documents or request information. The role is much more interesting than that usually termed as a receptionist and is certainly a lot more involved. For example, the first written report on a number of crimes is compiled at the front counter before it is submitted to the relevant department for action. This calls for the ability to gain clear and concise information from people who could very well be in a distressed state. A patient, level-headed and sympathetic attitude is required, together with maturity and common sense.

The sheer diversity of events and incidents that can occur in the course of any working day means that the job offers a great deal of variety. No two situations will ever be quite the same, so officers will need to display a considerable degree of initiative – police colleagues will be relying on them for vital support. As with all administrative posts, a methodical approach to paperwork is essential. Although contact with the public will be face to face or via the telephone, verbal information must be committed to paper in all cases, with all the relevant facts, before any police inquiry can commence.

As one of the few civilian staff roles that is performed entirely in the public eye, the appearance of station reception officers must at all times reflect the professionalism of the Service and so a corporate uniform is worn. They will also be required to work to a shift pattern for which an appropriate shift allowance is paid.

Detention Officers

Detention officers are responsible for receiving and processing prisoners. They may undertake searches, obtain fingerprints, photographs and DNA samples and issue medication in accordance with force guidelines. They also operate and maintain equipment and ensure that drug testing is carried out properly. They assist in the preparation and serving of meals and provide support in the custody area, escorting and restraining prisoners. Applicants should be physically fit, with an aptitude for computer work. This position is often suitable for job-share.

Clerical Assistants

This is the basic administrative grade (the job title varies across forces). All police activities are team-orientated and it is the job of clerical assistants to ensure that information shared by the team is properly documented and readily accessible. This could involve registering post, indexing reports, updating computer records, filing and photocopying, handling telephone inquiries, and processing mileage, travelling and subsistence claims as well as overtime payments. Applicants should be able to operate computerised databases and must be focused, well organised and responsible.

Day-to-day activities will largely depend upon where staff are posted. They could be part of a team at their local police station. Alternatively, they could be working in the unit that deals with the investigation of road traffic offences, or collating papers relating to criminal investigations for court. Other areas include personnel, finance and licensing.

Clerical Officers

The difference between the role of clerical officer and clerical assistant lies not in the type of work they will be involved with, but rather just how much involvement they want. The higher grade requires a responsible attitude to work that can at times be very demanding. Much of their time will be spent on paperwork, but there can be a great deal of contact with police officers, other civilian staff and members of the public. Like a clerical assistant, they will usually work as part of a small team under the direct control of an executive officer.

Clerical officers may find themselves working in a police station, area headquarters or branch. At a station, they might be involved with the investigation of road traffic offences or compiling criminal case documentation. They could be providing general administrative support or looking after property in the property office. At area headquarters, they could take on personnel-related duties for both police officers and civilian staff. Alternatively, they could end up working in one of the specialised departments or at a training college. This grade provides the opportunity to demonstrate a wide range of skills and ability. If potential and commitment is displayed, promotion to the management executive grade will follow.

Executive Officers

The police do not just offer careers for those who choose to specialise. They realise that there are highly qualified individuals with a much more generalist attitude to a career, keen to make their mark in a large organisation. There is a wealth of opportunity and a range of career options available – greater than in many commercial companies.

Executive officers are the first managers of civilian staff. As such, this post offers a leading role, building, supervising and motivating a team of clerical assistants and clerical officers, whether based at area headquarters, a branch or police station.

They could be involved with the monitoring of expenses and overtime budgets, or enabling secretarial support for the senior police and civilian staff management team. Alternatively, they may have to make recommendations on courses of action in the investigation of road traffic and criminal offences, or supervise case papers for court. All of this requires day-to-day liaison with police officers, headquarters departments, local authorities and members of the public – so good interpersonal skills are vital. At area headquarters or a branch, they could be in human resources, dealing with staff recruitment or appraisal and welfare, where they will be able to develop their organisational skills to the full. Other departments include media services, specialist operations and manpower planning. There are other many options for those interested in developing a computer specialisation, from systems analysis to technical support.

Whatever their involvement, being an executive officer opens a challenging new career chapter in which to develop existing skills. Recently, many posts formally held by police officers have been reassigned to civilian staff, which has greatly enhanced the variety of work and level of management responsibility across a wide range of activities.

Anyone who joins the Service as a clerical assistant or officer can aspire to the grade of executive officer through internal promotion. As promotion is on individual merit, via an internal assessment, there is no reason why someone with commitment and enthusiasm cannot reach a management grade.

Secretarial Staff

Communication plays a vital role within the Service and is dependent upon clarity and accuracy in all its forms. A secretary or typist working at a police station is likely to be dealing with a wide range of paperwork – anything from police officers' crime reports to statements from witnesses, senior management minutes of meetings, or correspondence from victims of crime.

Preparing a statement of evidence for court is often more than just a case of word-processing. Provided sometimes with just the basic information (usually with terrible handwriting), it is up to the secretarial staff to phrase it into correct English, without changing any of the essential facts. Area headquarters and branch postings are just as challenging, processing confidential reports relating to anything from serious fraud investigations to community partnership initiatives.

Applicants should have excellent word-processing computer skills, and a good command of English and spelling. The possession of shorthand and secretarial skills, plus good organisational and inter-personal skills, could put them in line for internal promotion to the role of personal secretary. Working directly for senior police and civilian staff management in the Service is very intensive.

Scientific Support Services

This department encompasses a variety of services that provide the necessary tools to aid the investigation of crime. These services can include a scenes of crime department, scientific aids laboratory, fingerprint bureau and a technical support unit. During the last few years there have been dramatic advances in DNA profiling and together with the national fingerprint database, scientific progress has revolutionised crime investigation.

The main function of scientific support is to collect and process forensic evidence recovered from the scene of a crime. Examination of this evidence will show if a crime has indeed been committed, whether there are any clues that point to the identity of the offender, and whether there is anything to link the offender to the scene. Examiners are trained to recover forensic trace evidence, such as fibres, paint and crime stains, which may have DNA material left at the scene by suspects. Footwear evidence is also increasingly important and detailed shoe patterns are examined. High-tech crime unit staff frequently seize and examine computers believed to be used in criminal activity.

Technical photographs are also important, because they accurately depict the scene, evidence or the victim's injuries. Technical support units provide police officers with the necessary equipment to carry out surveillance tasks. The police are becoming more and more reliant on scientific evidence to secure convictions in the courts of law. Applicants who have a science background will find this a fascinating career.

The National Training Centre for Scientific Support to Crime Investigation (NTCSSCI) trains police scientific support personnel in the UK. The Forensic Science Service (FSS) also offers training, consultancy and specialist assistance. FSS has over 1,000 trained scientists, many of whom are authorities in their fields. It used to be a public service but is now, as the Police Federation complains, a 'profit-driven organisation'.

Scenes of crime

Scenes of crime officers (SOCOs) collect vital evidence from the scene of the incident. This can include fingerprints, blood or weapons. They carefully package and store the relevant material to ensure it is kept in good condition before being sent off to the laboratory for DNA and other analysis. They also have to attend post mortem examinations, and appear in court and present evidence as required. SOCOs need accuracy and logic as well as excellent powers of observation and concentration.

Fingerprint Unit

Fingerprint examination of evidence recovered from the scene of crime is carried out both manually and by computer against a vast databank of prints obtained from convicted criminals. The fingerprint team examines traces recovered from the incident by the scenes of crime officer and enhance the more obscure marks in the laboratory. They use various techniques, either conventional powder treatment or chemical treatment processes.

The National Fingerprint Office (NFO) maintains the national fingerprint database of prints prior to 2001 in the National Fingerprint Archive. It has contacts with Interpol, the Scottish Criminal Record Office, the Prison Service and many other forces. From 2001 the responsibility for processing and storing their own prints was devolved to the Constabularies in England and Wales. The National Automated Fingerprint Identification System (NASIS) enables forces to rapidly search records.

Photographic Unit

The photographic unit is responsible for developing all the photographs taken by scenes of crime and operational officers. These may include victims' injuries as well as photographs recording the scene.

Video Unit

Some forces also have video units. The growing use of CCTV cameras in public places provides information for crime investigations. Staff use computerised equipment for enhancing relevant sections of the film. They also provide videos of scenes of major incidents and produce films for training and promotional work.

Identification and Vetting Services

In 1995 the Phoenix application was launched. It allowed forces around the country to create and update criminal records from their own computers. Prior to that date only the National Identification Service (NIS), based at New Scotland Yard, could enter data on the Police National Computer. NIS still maintains information prior to 1995 on microfilm, and police forces pay for computer access to these mature criminal records.

The Criminal Records Bureau (CRB) requests police forces to undertake local record checks on people seeking access to children and vulnerable adults. These people may be hoping to adopt or foster, or simply applying for a job. Different agencies around the country are involved with this process. In London, it is the staff at the Character Enquiry Centre based at New Scotland Yard. Employees at the National Security Vetting Office carry out Police National Computer searches on behalf of government agencies, and vet employees who may be applying to work in sensitive areas.

The Telephone Section at New Scotland Yard supplies phone and postal information from police records to Police Services in England and Wales. They are also occasionally approached by police from Northern

Ireland, Scotland and the Channel Islands, the courts, Immigration Services, Interpol and Child Protection Teams, who rely on the section for specific information relating to individuals who may be a risk to children. The Telephone Section provides the offender's antecedents, identification details, associates and last known address. The Immigration Services use the services of this unit to inform their deportation teams.

The National Identification Service Intelligence Section (NISIS) combines a criminal database searching agency and the Police Gazette (the central publication agency for UK police) to provide criminal intelligence and publication facilities at a national level.

Technology Services

There are many specialist engineering posts available (if you have the appropriate qualifications), providing police departments with technical and operational support of the highest standard.

The spread of expertise covers: data communications, associated computer systems, telecommunications, audio-visual services, protection technology against ballistic or explosive attacks, navigation aids, secure processing and analysis for electronic devices and storage media, airborne avionics, radio systems planning, fingerprint recognition systems, marine engineering, and maintaining fleets of motor vehicles, boats, aircraft and helicopters, etc.

Highly efficient computer systems are vitally important in the modern Police Service. The system known as 'Holmes' was developed by the Police Information Technology Organisation (PITO) after the Yorkshire Ripper enquiry. There was such a vast quantity of information collected and stored, that it became impossible for any one person to have a complete overview. Holmes not only automated the process of collecting and collating the information, but also enabled the investigation to be conducted in an organised manner. Holmes 2 is currently being developed.

Other areas where electronic engineering expertise is currently utilised include hi-tech security systems and specialised technical services supporting operational officers involved in sensitive casework. For example, PITO, which is a public body, provides IT and communications systems and services to the police and other criminal justice organisations in the United Kingdom. In London, the Operational and Technical Support Unit (OTSU) provides technical support for the Metropolitan Police and is part of C3I, a command, control, communications and information project. OTSU provides front line operational technical support to police officers, and evidential audio-visual analysis, together with electronic, computer and security protection, vehicle location, public CCTV, night camera and counter-terrorism systems, etc.

Technical experts are often called on to act as expert witnesses in court. They liaise with Specialist Operations in the Metropolitan Police, plus the National Crime Squad (NCS), the National Criminal Intelligence Service (NCIS), Customs and Excise and the security services. From time to time they also accompany police officers overseas on international drugs operations.

Communication Services

All forces today are acquiring fully integrated information and communications systems, which greatly improve police effectiveness. Communications technology nowadays is flexible and efficient, combining call handling, emergency and non-emergency contact, and command and control functions, allowing police to deal with ever-increasing requests for assistance.

Currently the mmO$_2$ consortium is expanding the new £2.9 billion 'Airwave' digital police radio system (which delivers clear reception, secure fully encrypted voice transmission and greater radio coverage) into 25 more force areas in the UK. It intends to cover the whole country by 2005. Airwave is based on the Tetra (terrestrial trunked radio) system, and there have been huge concerns about the long-term health effects, both on officers using the system and residents living near the Tetra masts. There have also been concerns about the cost of the project and it has been called a 'monstrous muddle'. The Home Office insists the system is safe, but to be sure is spending £5 million on research, and a study will be commissioned from Imperial College in London. Officers already using the system in 26 forces will be monitored, as will the general public in the affected areas. Airwave network is also intended for the emergency services, the military and some private companies.

Apart from the normal call centre and control room, which is a vital part of any police station, each force has a central operations room where 999 calls are received and information fed out to the local patrol cars and stations. One of many functions of the operations room is to be ready to deal with a major incident, such as a bomb, a plane crash, a derailment, or a major street riot. The operations room has the facilities to set up operational control points on the spot with mobile major incident vehicles.

To work in communications employees need to be calm and have the ability to work under pressure. A clear speaking voice is obviously an asset. Traditionally, experienced police officers have staffed it, although civilians are now employed, usually under the supervision of a serving officer. Whether answering a 999 emergency call from a member of the public, or dealing with urgent requests for information, communications staff provide a vital coordinating link within the Service.

Staff may be stationed at a regional command and control complex, or in the control room of a police station. Based in any one of these nerve centres, they will be receiving and relaying messages as well as obtaining the necessary information to enable police inquiries to be initiated. They may also be required to direct available manpower to the scene of an incident, provide advice and guidance where necessary and make detailed records. Whatever the situation, they will be relied upon for their ability to make swift and clear-headed decisions.

Good interpersonal skills are also an essential quality, as some callers to the emergency service may be in a highly distressed state. How well staff assess an emergency and acquire all the information, is reflected in the speed of the police response! As the role requires a high level of technical knowledge, comprehensive training will be given, so previous experience in this field is not strictly necessary. Communications staff operate a 24-hour shift pattern, for which an appropriate shift allowance is paid.

Estate Services

Forces across the country own a large estate of property, including individual police stations, plus residential accommodation and operational buildings such as offices, garages, workshops, gymnasiums and even boatyards.

Overall responsibility for this huge estate, involving provision, design, maintenance and disposal, lies with a wide range of specialists, often working in multi-discipline teams. In architecture, surveying, estates management, public health, mechanical, and electrical engineering, the Police Service offers good career opportunities.

Media Services

Most forces have a press office, or it may be called media services, or even public relations. Applicants with previous experience in this field are preferred. Staff in this department of the Police Service liaise closely with the media (television, radio, national and local papers) to make sure they are aware of policing issues such as appeals for information on recent crimes. The vital role that the media plays in communicating with the public is recognised and exploited. It is usually the headquarters press office that deals with enquiries about area issues, major and serious crime, police policy and queries about serious incidents on the roads. The force Web site is used as a means of informing local people about the latest initiatives, such as 'Bag-a-Burglar', 'Car Watch', 'Farm Watch' or 'Crackdown on Drugs', and encouraging them to make their opinions known – 'Have Your Say'. 'Publication services' is a section that may also be combined with the media unit. It produces internal and external magazines, brochures and leaflets for the Service.

OTHER SERVICES

If you think that the choice of civilian jobs is bewildering, the examples given are just the tip of the iceberg. The Police Service is a gigantic organisation and the following departments also present job opportunities in some but not all of the forces across the country. The list will at least give you an idea about the size of the club that you are thinking about joining:

Marketing	Transport
Supplies	Catering
Accounting	Financial Systems Development
Central Statistics	Legal Services
Outsourcing	Risk Management
Operational Policy and Support	Crime Analysis
Education and Development	Occupational Health and Welfare
Corporate Diversity	Management Policy Planning and
Health and Safety	Performance
Human Resources	Internal Investigations

EMPLOYMENT CONDITIONS

Training for civilian staff

Generally, induction training for clerical grades takes place with the aid of desk training manuals under the guidance of the line manager and help from team colleagues. This enables newcomers to gain vital hands-on experience right from the start. However, employees employed on work of a technical nature can expect to be given training in their particular field. Local training may be supplemented by specialist courses at training establishments for certain subjects. If staff demonstrate promotion potential, they will be given the opportunity to undergo developmental training. Management training automatically follows promotion.

Benefits

In most roles staff will be generally expected to work a 41-hour week (inclusive of lunch breaks), but most departments operate a flexible-working pattern for the benefit of staff. There are also increasing opportunities for job-sharing and part-time working. Fixed-term contracts also apply to some posts.

Benefits include maternity support and adoption leave, as well as a career break scheme. Some forces include interest-free season ticket loans and subsidised catering facilities. There are also extensive sports and social facilities throughout the Service that cater for most of the usual indoor and outdoor sports and recreations.

Salaries are enhanced by local weighting and shift allowances dependent on the working pattern and location. Usually 22 days' annual leave is awarded on joining, rising to 25 days after one year's service and supplemented by a further 10½ days' public and privilege leave. Applicants should check the details with the force on application.

Application

You can find out about current recruitment by logging on to the relevant force Web site or by contacting the Human Resources Department at your local police station. Check local press regularly for recruitment advertisements, as well as the Job Centres. Vacancies at headquarters buildings for management executive vacancies are sometimes advertised in both regional and national press.

11

Specials

ARE YOU SPECIAL?

Demands on the Police Service are increasing, and all the forces in the country have their own Special Constabularies, sometimes comprising as much as a quarter of their strength. On recruitment you will receive comprehensive training, so that you are competent to help regular officers with the task of providing an essential service to the community.

If you are thinking about applying, you should consider the following 10 points to see if the work of a 'Special' is likely to suit you:

1. The position is voluntary – apart from expenses, you receive no salary.

2. It is not a hobby.

3. Training and on-the-job experience will equip you with valuable new skills.

4. You need to show a willingness to learn and the ability to think clearly.

5. You must be dedicated, responsible, tolerant, impartial and public spirited.

6. The work is not always easy, but is enjoyable, varied and challenging.

7. The job enables you to give something back to the community.

8. You are offered a complete change to your normal lifestyle.

9. There is the opportunity to make lasting friendships and develop team spirit.

10. You can join the Sports and Social Club at your station.

Application

There are other factors you have to consider before you put in your application. Briefly, the terms and conditions are:

- You should be aged between 18½ and 50.

- Your nationality should meet the eligibility standards in Chapter 1.

- You are expected to dedicate a minimum of 16 hours per month to the job, but also be prepared to be flexible and do night shifts as well as day shifts.

- Duties are arranged to fit in with your work and home commitments, but in emergencies you should attend for duty when summoned.

- You are asked to regard it as a long-term commitment – for at least two years.

- You will be on probation for one year.

- You must be of good character and not be an associate of known criminals.

- Disciplinary procedures will be invoked if you break the rules of conduct.

- You must be fit and healthy – certain medical conditions may preclude you.

- Your eyesight should meet the eligibility standards in Chapter 1.

- You must declare cautions/convictions, including from military authorities.

- Certain occupations may be incompatible with your job as a Special, since they may put you in a compromising position. These include: member of the armed forces, private or store detective, security or court escort officer, court clerk or magistrate, traffic warden, or member of a police authority.

- You will not receive a salary, but will be reimbursed for all expenses incurred in carrying out your duties (payment for hours worked is under discussion though).

- All uniform is provided free of charge, plus uniform cleaning vouchers.

- You must be of good character and enquiries are made with personal referees.

There are a series of stages that you have to undergo when you apply for the Special Constabulary. Firstly, your application form is carefully studied to see if it meets all the criteria. Then you are required to take an entrance test, and a selection board interviews you at the local police station. Finally, your medical questionnaire is carefully checked and you are given a physical examination. When these are satisfactorily completed, you can commence your initial training.

Training

At the end of the recruitment stages, you start on the initial training course, which usually takes place over six weekends at force headquarters. Police procedure and law are taught, including powers of arrest, details of common offences, taking prisoners into custody, using a notebook, filling in statements and forms to a high standard, and using a police radio, etc. Later you will receive instruction in unarmed defence, using your baton, handcuffs and CS or pepper spray, followed by a practical and written exam authorising you to carry and use protection equipment. You will have to continue your training with monthly sessions on division and a couple of weekend courses at headquarters during your first year, which will probably include classes on firearms awareness and counter-terrorism.

You will begin your duties as soon as you have completed your training course, but for the first 12 months of your service you will be on probation and following an intensive practical programme. During the first few months, an experienced tutor officer will monitor your progress. After that you will begin your normal duties alongside your colleagues.

When you have completed your probationary period, you are invested as a constable with full powers at an attestation ceremony, which takes place at force headquarters (members of your family are welcome to attend). Then you are ready to go out on independent patrol, although for most of the time you will be working with another officer beside you. Most Specials work within the area in which they live, but you can request to work elsewhere if you wish.

DUTIES

You will have the same powers as a regular police officer and wear a similar uniform. Under supervision, your role will be mainly routine patrol work at weekends, either on the beat or in a police vehicle. This is an important service since it provides a visible uniformed presence on the streets and acts as a deterrent. Friday nights outside pubs and clubs and

Saturdays in shopping centres are the busiest times for the police and your assistance really makes a difference. You will also be on the lookout for anti-social behaviour in residential areas, helping to improve the quality of life for the community, and possibly conducting vandalism patrols around school grounds.

The task of neighbourhood Special Constable is a popular choice. You need an expert knowledge of the area in which you are working, so that you can act as a bridge between residents, schools and businesses on the one hand, and the police on the other. Your aim is to build trust and confidence within the community, and you will learn a lot about life and human nature.

In the course of your duties you may be involved with the following activities: crime prevention work, schools liaison, dealing with under-age drinking, property marking programmes; public order offences, criminal damage, house-to-house enquiries, carrying out observations, assisting with accidents and fires, road safety initiatives, recording details of road accidents, enforcing traffic legislation, safeguarding public safety at local or major events such as sports matches or festivals, and presenting evidence in court.

New skills

As a Special you are sure to acquire new and develop existing skills that will stand you in good stead for the rest of your life. You will find you can cope with the unexpected and stay calm in a crisis. Resolving disputes with tact and quick thinking will be learnt, as will clear communication and inter-personal skills. These talents will help you in your daily life as well as in your regular job. Self-respect and confidence are bound to grow as you successfully tackle more difficult problems.

Once you have been in the job for a couple of years, you may consider applying for promotion, which will require more hours and a greater degree of commitment. You will have to appear before a promotion board. The ranks above Special Constable in the Constabularies are: Section Officer, Divisional Officer, Divisional Commandant, and County Commandant.

12

Police associations

Police may not join a trade union or take part in politics, and must at all times obey the lawful orders of their senior officers. However, there are several associations that they can belong to that will support them and provide advice and assistance.

POLICE FEDERATION

The Police Federation of England and Wales was established by the Police Act in 1919 and has a membership of around 130,000. It is the statutory organisation that is responsible for representing its members in all matters affecting welfare and efficiency. All the elected officials of the Police Federation must be serving police officers. There are separate Police Federations for Scotland and Northern Ireland. The Federation does not represent 'non-Home Office' police forces, for example, British Transport, Ministry of Defence, Isle of Man, etc, which have their own organisations.

Police officers pay voluntary contributions to the Federation. The funds raised provide services to members, such as financial backing and free legal and medical advice. This enables them to pursue civil claims for injuries from accidents or criminal assault, or for defamation and equal opportunity cases. The Federation provides legal advice to members who are charged with certain criminal offences arising wholly from the course of their duties, and for those facing serious disciplinary allegations – although it should not be assumed that the Federation is backing a member facing charges.

Representatives from the Police Federation also attend the Police Negotiating Board (PNB), which is the statutory negotiating body for police pay and conditions of service in the UK.

The current chairman is Mrs Jan Berry of Kent Police. She is the first woman chairperson in the history of the Police Federation. Her service has been spent mainly on operational duties within the county. She became a local Federation representative in 1987 and was elected chairman in 2002. Her main aims are 'to improve the professionalism of the police service, enhance police training and achieve greater inclusiveness within the Federation'.

ASSOCIATION OF CHIEF POLICE OFFICERS

The Association of Chief Police Officers (ACPO) is the corporate voice of the Service, promoting excellence in leadership, providing professional opinion on key issues of the policing agenda, such as crime, race, community relations, personnel concerns, road policing and performance management. ACPO works closely with a wide range of agencies in government, the other emergency services and the voluntary and private sectors. It cannot tell chief constables what to do – it simply formulates policy guidance documents recommending appropriate action.

The members of ACPO are police officers who hold the rank of chief constable, deputy chief constable or assistant chief constable (or their equivalents) within the forces of England, Wales and Northern Ireland, national police agencies and other forces in the UK and Channel Islands. Some senior civilians are also members.

It is not a staff association – there is a separate Chief Police Officers' Association (CPOSA) for that. ACPO works on behalf of the Service, rather than its own members. It has the status of a private company, conforms to company law and has a Board of Directors. It is funded by a combination of Home Office grant, contributions from the police authorities and subscriptions. Ten Business Areas manage the various strategies. ACPO produces publications on policy issues such as drugs, alcohol, asylum seekers, road policing, disability, hate crime, DNA, information technology, Airwave, corruption, and the Macpherson Report on the Lawrence case, etc. It also provides leadership guidance, promotes a professional and ethical service, liaises with government in civil emergencies, and provides professional advice to police authorities and other organisations.

POLICE SUPERINTENDENTS' ASSOCIATION

The Police Superintendents' Association of England and Wales represents the superintending ranks on issues affecting their welfare and efficiency. Superintendents are not members of the Police Federation.

NATIONAL BLACK POLICE ASSOCIATION

The National Black Police Association was formed in 1999. It helps the Police Service deliver a fair and equitable service to all sections of the community. It also aims to improve the working environment of black staff, by protecting their rights and enhancing racial harmony and the quality of service to the minority ethnic community.

GAY POLICE ASSOCIATION

Gay and lesbian police employees represent the largest minority group in the Police Service. The Gay Police Association promotes equal opportunities for lesbian and gay Police Service employees, offering advice and support to employees.

ASSOCIATION OF WOMEN POLICE

The Association of Women Police represents employees from all ranks of the Police Service including support staff. It was formed to enhance the specific role of women within the Service. It was founded in 1987.

POLICE AUTHORITIES

Although not a police association, police authorities are organisations that work in partnership with their local force and hold them to account for the service they provide. There are police authorities linked to most of the forces in the UK. They are independent bodies made up of local people and their job is to ensure the force is efficient and effective in reducing crime and disorder and the fear of crime. Police authorities consult with the community, engage in constructive local partnerships, set local policing priorities, produce annual and strategic plans, set the force budget and decide how much of it is raised through the local council tax, they also appoint the chief constable and other senior police staff, and monitor complaints against the police.

13

Police services

POLICE SERVICE IN ENGLAND AND WALES

There are 43 police forces in England and Wales – mainly County Constabularies and some metropolitan/city forces. London has two forces of its own. There is talk of amalgamating some of the forces, but no decision has yet been taken.

Avon & Somerset
Cambridgeshire
City of London
Cumbria
Devon & Cornwall
Durham
Essex
Greater Manchester
Hampshire
Humberside
Lancashire
Lincolnshire
Metropolitan
Northamptonshire
North Wales
Nottinghamshire
South Yorkshire
Suffolk
Sussex
Warwickshire
West Midlands
Wiltshire

Bedfordshire
Cheshire
Cleveland
Derbyshire
Dorset
Dyfed-Powys
Gloucestershire
Gwent
Hertfordshire
Kent
Leicestershire
Merseyside
Norfolk
Northumbria
North Yorkshire
South Wales
Staffordshire
Surrey
Thames Valley
West Mercia
West Yorkshire

Metropolitan Police

The Metropolitan Police Service is the largest force in the country. Sir Robert Peel founded it in 1829. The original force of 1,000 officers policed a population of less than 2 million. Now it serves over 7 million residents in 33 individual boroughs plus around 1 million daily commuters. The force now employs over 29,000 officers, over 11,000 civilian staff, over 600 traffic wardens and just under 900 Police Community Support Officers. It must respond to some 2 million emergency 999 calls each year, which is a formidable task.

London is divided into several policing areas, each sector about the size of a complete force elsewhere in the country. Since 2000, the Metropolitan Police Service has been accountable to the Metropolitan Police Authority.

City of London Police

The City of London Police force is, for historical reasons, a self-governing body. It is the smallest UK force with around 1,200 staff, and covers 'the square mile' of the City of London, which has around 6,000 residents, plus several hundreds of thousands of daily commuters. There are six command areas and two territorial divisions – Bishopsgate and Snow Hill.

OTHER FORCES

There are many other specialised and local forces across the country, which do not come under direct control of the Home Office. They include the British Transport Police, Ministry of Defence Police, Isle of Man Constabulary, Jersey Police, Guernsey Police, Royal Botanic Gardens Constabulary, Royal Parks Constabulary, Borough Parks Police, and the UK Atomic Authority Constabulary. Here are descriptions of just a few of them.

British Transport Police

British Transport Police (BTP) started in 1826 on the Stockton and Darlington Railway and is consequently one of the oldest police forces in the world. The Railway Police were among the first to recruit women to their ranks, and in 1908 the North Eastern Railway Police pioneered the use of police dogs. BTP is responsible for policing Britain's railways. The force has nearly 3,000 officers and civilian support staff employed across the entire rail network, including London Underground, Docklands Light Railway, the Midland Metro and Croydon Tramlink.

Every day over a quarter of a million tons of freight move around the network, from factories and freight depots to docks. Additionally

5 million passenger journeys are made daily. The British Transport Police must ensure that all this takes place within a safe environment. Many members of the force have been honoured for their bravery and courage, for instance at the Underground fire at Kings Cross.

Criminals can readily cross county and national boundaries, enabling crimes to be committed on the move with rapid means of escape (on Eurostar for example). Thousands of offences are reported to the force each year, ranging from minor public order offences to serious assaults, dangerous obstructions on the rails, and even terrorism and murder. Officers have to deal with a huge number of calls for help, tracking down missing children, investigating theft of personal property, and crowd control of football fans, etc.

Successful candidates must undergo the full national police-training programme. British Transport Police are on the same pay scales as most other police officers.

Ministry of Defence Police

The Ministry of Defence Police (MDP) is an executive agency of the Ministry of Defence (MoD). In 1996 it became an Agency, led by a Chief Constable and assisted by an Agency Management Board.

MDP is the MoD's dedicated civil police force, and consists of approximately 3,400 officers and 300 civil servants. They operate out of MoD establishments throughout the country and are the UK's only truly national police force. Every officer is weapons-trained and 70 per cent of officers on duty carry arms. They are deployed at around 120 sites, and guard Britain's nuclear deterrent. The police also have responsibility for the dockyards, and marine units have a large number of inflatable boats and launches at their disposal. Liaison with Customs and Excise is close, and they stop and search sea-going vessels for drugs and contraband. Some 400 handlers work with specially trained police dogs that sniff out explosives, arms or drugs.

There is a Criminal Investigation Department and a Fraud Squad. 50 Operational Support Unit (OSU) officers can be deployed anywhere in the UK at short notice, and perform public order duties and anti-terrorist searches, etc. Officers escort and protect deliveries of nuclear material between MoD establishments. As well as MoD sites, they police USAF bases, Defence Research Establishments, Royal Ordnance Factories and the Royal Mint. Police also attend public events such as the Farnborough International Air Show, the Army Equipment Exhibition at Aldershot, the Fairford Air Tattoo, and the start of the Cutty Sark Tall Ships race, among many other activities. The Anti Terrorism, Crime and Security Act 2001 extends their jurisdiction beyond the MoD estate if necessary. MDP's headquarters is at Wethersfield, a former US air force base, which has a two-mile runway. Interested applicants should view the MDP Web site (see Chapter 14).

Royal Parks Constabulary

The Royal Parks Constabulary (RPC) dates back to 1872, when the Parks Regulation Act created a force of Royal Park Keepers, with all the powers of police constables. In 1974 it became the Royal Parks Constabulary, which is now accountable to the Department for Culture, Media and Sport, not the Home Office.

The police patrol in 17 distinct locations in and around London, including the eight Royal Parks and a number of public gardens, covering over 6,000 acres that are visited by millions of people every year. The RPC ensures that the grounds remain free from disturbance and the public free from the fear of crime. There are permanent units of mounted police, dog handlers and motor cycle officers at several of the London parks 24 hours a day, 7 days a week. Currently there are discussions being held about merging with the Metropolitan Police.

UK Atomic Energy Authority Constabulary

The UK Atomic Energy Authority Constabulary (UKAEAC) was set up in 1954 and has fewer than 600 officers. It is accountable to Parliament through the Department of Trade and Industry. Its main role is to provide a secure working environment at all UKAEA nuclear sites and those of BNFL (British Nuclear Fuels) and URENCO. The police are responsible for the protection of nuclear materials both on the sites and in transit. The Directorate of Civil Nuclear Security provides independent regulation.

UKAEAC officers are trained to the highest standard including the use of firearms. Officers at each location have a close working relationship with their opposite numbers in the local police force. Apart from guarding nuclear facilities, the police carry out a normal role, in other words, prevention of crime, detection and arrest of offenders, protection of life and property and the maintenance of the Queen's Peace.

The operational area includes the premises of UKAEA and BNFL – up to a radius of 15 miles. Force headquarters and the communication centre are based at the UKAEA's Culham site. The Constabulary Training Centre is located at Summergrove in Cumbria. The force consists of seven operational units, each headed by an inspector, chief inspector or superintendent, depending on the responsibilities involved. Officers have to be in a constant state of readiness because of potential terrorist threats to nuclear installations.

SCOTTISH POLICE SERVICE

There are eight forces in Scotland:

Central Scotland Police	Dumfries & Galloway Constabulary
Fife Constabulary	Grampian Police
Lothian & Borders Police	Northern Constabulary
Strathclyde Police	Tayside Police

The basic criteria for applicants wishing to join the Scottish Police Service are basically the same as for England and Wales. Contact the relevant force for full details (see Chapter 14 for Web site addresses).

Each force's selection process involves a standard entrance examination, interview, fitness and medical tests, as well as background inquiries. If you have gained a degree, however, you may want to apply for the Accelerated Promotion Scheme for Graduates (APSG). Testing for this takes place at the beginning of each year, and if you pass through the standard entrance test with good results, you will proceed to a force selection board. Then if selected, you will attend an assessment interview at the Scottish Police College, which includes practical tests. If you perform well, you will be accepted as a recruit on the Accelerated Promotion Scheme, which as the name implies is the fast-track promotion route through the Service. If you fail, don't worry, it is very likely that you will still be accepted under the standard entry conditions.

The standard entrance test covers language, information handling and number work. You are allowed a maximum of three attempts to pass and may have to wait for six months before being allowed to resit. Once your background have been checked, you are invited to a one-day assessment course. As part of the course you will have to undergo a medical examination and fitness testing. After that you will face an interview panel. Even if you are not accepted by one particular force, you can still apply to others.

The Scottish Police College is located in the centre of Scotland, situated in about 90 acres of parkland. At the heart of the campus is Tulliallan Castle, built in the early 19th century. It currently provides approximately three-quarters of all police and support staff training, from recruits to command level, including specialist training for detectives and traffic officers.

After the 12-week basic training course, whether you are an APSG or a standard entrant, you will return to your force and go out on patrol and work shifts. A tutor constable will accompany you at first, but then you will patrol on your own. After approximately 12 months' service, you will return to the College for a six-week advanced training course that will cover academic and theoretical matters.

During your probationary period back at the station, you will have to cope with a variety of tasks – attending accidents, searching for missing children, dealing with offences and making arrests, interviewing suspects or taking statements from witnesses, escorting prisoners, preparing crime reports, or attending court to give evidence.

If you would like details of the Scottish forces, see Chapter 14 or visit the Scottish Police Service Web site: www.scottish.police.uk.

POLICE SERVICE OF NORTHERN IRELAND

The Independent Commission on Policing in Northern Ireland was established in 1998 as a result of the Good Friday Agreement. Subsequently, the Police (Northern Ireland) Act 2000 came into force and the Police Service of Northern Ireland (PSNI) was inaugurated in 2001. The PSNI is responsible to the Northern Ireland Policing Board, which holds the Chief Constable to account for the force's performance against the targets. The Independent Commission proposed changes to the composition of the Service, and also to the recruitment process, which should be carried out by professional organisations. Police applicants must now submit their forms via an agency called Consensia (see Chapter 14 for address), and civilian applicants through Grafton Recruitment. Note that you can only request an application form from Consensia in March or September of each year, following advertisements in the press.

Prior to the establishment of the PSNI the police force was the Royal Ulster Constabulary (RUC), supported by the RUC Reserve, traffic wardens and civilian staff. Policing in Northern Ireland was governed by the 'tripartite structure' – the three agencies involved being the Secretary of State for Northern Ireland, the Police Authority for Northern Ireland and the Chief Constable of the RUC. Growing out of a police force that had been operating in Northern Ireland since 1822, the Royal Ulster Constabulary was formed in 1922. It grew into the second largest force in the UK, next to the Metropolitan Police in London. From the beginning, the RUC had a dual role, unique among United Kingdom police forces, of providing a traditional law enforcement Police Service, whilst at the same time protecting Northern Ireland from terrorists. Its members were armed and had the support of the Ulster Special Constabulary, a volunteer body of part-time trained auxiliary police.

RUC officers received many awards for gallantry over the years, which reflected the dangers they had to face. Awards since 1969 included 16 George Medals, 103 Queen's Gallantry Medals, 111 Queen's Commendations for Brave Conduct, and 69 Queen's Police Medals. In the 25 years between 1969 and 1994, 195 RUC and 101 RUC Reserve members were killed and over 7,000 injured.

Both the British and Irish governments hope that terrorist organisations in Northern Ireland have come to the realisation that their aims cannot be achieved by violence. Continued cross-security cooperation is vital in the fight against terrorism, and government and police are determined to end terrorism once and for all.

The Police Service in the province has undergone large-scale reforms and modernisation to ensure that it is sensitive to local needs and truly representative of the community it serves, in terms of both Catholic and Protestant employees. Specialist police units have been set up to tackle serious crime, such as terrorism, drug offences, domestic violence, stolen cars and traffic violations. There are some 3,000 civilian staff in the support sections and in administration, leaving police officers free to concentrate on their primary task of tackling crime.

14

Contact addresses

POLICE SERVICE IN ENGLAND AND WALES (Web site: www.police.uk)

Avon & Somerset Constabulary, PO Box 37, Valley Road, Portishead, Bristol BS20 8QJ; Tel: 01275 818181, Web site: www.avonandsomerset.police.uk

Bedfordshire Police, Woburn Road, Kempston, MK43 9AX; Tel: 01234 841212, Web site: www.bedfordshire.police.uk

Cambridgeshire Constabulary, Hinchingbrooke Park, Huntingdon PE29 6NP; Tel: 01480 456111, Web site: www.cambs-police.co.uk

Cheshire Constabulary, Castle Esplanade, Chester CHI 2PP; Tel: 01244 350000, Web site: www.cheshire.police.uk

Cleveland Constabulary, PO Box 70, Ladgate Lane, Middlesbrough TS8 9EH; Tel: 01642 326326, Web site: www.cleveland.police.uk

Cumbria Constabulary, Carleton Hall, Penrith CA10 2AU; Tel: 01768 891999, Web site: www.cumbria.police.uk

Derbyshire Constabulary, Butterley Hall, Ripley, DE5 3RS; Tel: 01773 570100, Web site: www.derbyshire.police.uk

Devon & Cornwall Constabulary, Middlemoor, Exeter EX2 7HQ; Tel: 08452 777444, Web site: www.devon-cornwall.police.uk

Dorset Police, Winfrith, Dorchester DT2 8DZ; Tel: 01929 462727, Web site: www.dorset.police.uk

Durham Constabulary, Aykley Heads, Durham DH1 5TT; Tel: 0191 3864929, Web site: www.durham.police.uk

Dyfed-Powys Police, PO Box 99, Carmarthen SA3I 2PF; Tel: 01267 232000, Web site: www.dyfed-powys.police.uk

Essex Police, PO Box 2. Springfield, Chelmsford CM2 6DA; Tel: 01245 491491, Web site: www.essex.police.uk

Gloucestershire Constabulary, Holland House, Lansdown Road, Cheltenham GL51 6QH (relocating shortly to Waterwells, Quedgeley); Tel: 0845 0901234, Web site: www.gloucestershire.police.uk

Greater Manchester Police, PO Box 22, Manchester MI6 0RE; Tel: 0161 872 5050, Web site: www.gmp.police.uk

Gwent Constabulary, Croesyceiliog, Cwmbran NP44 2XJ; Tel: 01633 838111, Web site: www.gwent.police.uk

Hampshire Constabulary, West Hill, Winchester, SO22 5DB; Tel: 0845 0454545, Web site: www.hampshire.police.uk

Hertfordshire Constabulary, Stanborough Road, Welwyn Garden City AL8 6XF; Tel: 01707 354000, Web site: www.herts.police.uk

Humberside Police, Priory Police Station, Kingston-upon-Hull HU5 5SF; Tel: 01482 326111, Web site: www.humberside.police.uk

Kent County Constabulary, Sutton Road, Maidstone MEI5 9BZ; Tel: 01622 690690, Web site: www.kent.police.uk

Lancashire Constabulary, PO Box 77, Hutton, Preston PR4 5SB; Tel: 0845 1253545, Web site: www.lancashire.police.uk

Leicestershire Constabulary, St John's, Enderby, Leicester LE19 2BX; Tel: 0116 222 2222, Web site: www.leics.police.uk

Lincolnshire Police, PO Box 999, Lincoln LN5 7PH; Tel: 01522 532222, Web site: www.lincs.police.uk

London, City Of London Police, 37 Wood Street, London EC2P 2NQ; Tel: 020 7601 2455, Web site: www.cityoflondon.police.uk

London, Metropolitan Police, New Scotland Yard, Broadway, London SW1H 0BG; Tel: 020 7230 1212, Web site: www.met.police.uk

Merseyside Police, PO Box 59, Liverpool L69 1JD; Tel: 0151 7096010, Web site: www.merseyside.police.uk

Norfolk Constabulary, Falconers Chase, Wymondham, NR18 0WW; Tel: 01953 424242, Web site: www.norfolk.police.uk

North Wales Police, Glan-y-Don, Colwyn Bay, Conwy, LL29 8AW; Tel: 08456 071002, Web site: www.north-wales.police.uk

North Yorkshire Police, Newby Wiske, Northallerton DL7 9HA; Tel: 01609 783131, Web site: www.northyorkshire.police.uk

Northamptonshire Police, Wootton Hall, Northampton NN4 0JQ; Tel: 01604 700700, Web site: www.northants.police.uk

Northumbria Police, Ponteland, Newcastle upon Tyne NE20 0BL; Tel: 01661 872555, Web site: www.northumbria.police.uk

Nottinghamshire Constabulary, Sherwood Lodge, Arnold, Nottingham NG5 8PP; Tel: 0115 967 0999, Web site: www.nottinghamshire.police.uk

South Wales Constabulary, Bridgend CF3I 3SU; Tel: 01656 655555, Web site: www.south-wales.police.uk

South Yorkshire Police, Snig Hill, Sheffield S3 8LY; Tel: 0114 220 2020, Web site: www.southyorks.police.uk

Staffordshire Police, Cannock Road, Stafford ST17 0QG; Tel: 01785 257717, Web site: www.staffordshire.police.uk

Suffolk Constabulary, Martlesham Heath, Ipswich IP5 3QS; Tel: 01473 613500, Web site: www.suffolk.police.uk

Surrey Police, Mount Browne, Sandy Lane, Guildford GU3 IHG; Tel: 0845 1252222, Web site: www.surrey.police.uk

Sussex Police, Church Lane, Lewes BN7 2DZ; Tel: 0845 6070 999, Web site: www.sussex.police.uk

Thames Valley Police, Oxford Road, Kidlington, Oxfordshire, 2NX; Tel: 08458 505505, Web site: www.thamesvalley.police.uk

Warwickshire Constabulary, PO Box 4, Leek Wootton, Warwick CV35 7QB; Tel: 01926 415000, Web site: www.warwickshire. police.uk

West Mercia Constabulary, Hindlip Hall, Hindlip, PO Box 55, Worcester WR3 8SP; Tel: 08457 444888, Web site: www.westmercia.police.uk

West Midlands Police, Lloyd House, Colmore Circus, Birmingham B4 6NQ; Tel: 0845 1135000, Web site: www.west-midlands.police.uk

West Yorkshire Police, PO Box 9, Wakefield WF1 3QP; Tel: 0845 6060606, Web site: www.westyorkshire.police.uk

Wiltshire Constabulary, London Road, Devizes SN10 2DN; Tel: 01380 722341, Web site: www.wiltshire.police.uk

SCOTTISH POLICE SERVICE (Web site: www.scottish.police.uk)

Central Scotland Police, Randolphfield, Stirling FK8 2HD; Tel: 01786 456000, Web site: www.centralscotland.police.uk

Dumfries & Galloway Constabulary, Cornwall Mount, Dumfries DG1 1PZ; Tel: 01387 252112, Web site: www.dumfriesand galloway.police.uk

Fife Constabulary, Detroit Road, Glenrothes, KY6 2RJ; Tel: 01592 418888, Web site: www.fife.police.uk

Grampian Police, Queen Street, Aberdeen AB10 1ZA; Tel: 0845 6005700, Web site: www.grampian.police.uk

Lothian & Borders Police, Fettes Avenue, Edinburgh EH4; Tel: 0131 311 3131, Web site: www.lpb.police.uk

Northern Constabulary, Perth Road, Inverness IV2 3SY; Tel: 01463 715555, Web site: www.northern.police.uk

Strathclyde Police, 173 Pitt Street, Glasgow G2 4JS; Tel: 01415 322000, Web site:www.strathclyde.police.uk

Tayside Police, PO Box 59, West Bell Street, Dundee DD1 9JU; Tel: 01382 223200, Web site: www.tayside.police.uk

POLICE SERVICE OF NORTHERN IRELAND

Police Service of Northern Ireland, Knock Road, Belfast BT5 6LE; Tel: 02890 650222, Web site: www.psni.police.uk

OTHER FORCES

British Transport Police, PO Box 260, 15 Tavistock Place, London WC1H 9SJ; Tel: 020 7830 8854, Web site: www.btp.police.uk

Epping Forest (Forest Keepers), Conservator of Epping Forest, Corporation of London, The Warren, Loughton, Essex IG10 4RW; Tel: 020 8508 2266, no Web site

Guernsey Police, Hospital Lane, St. Peter Port GY1 2QN; Tel: 01481 725111, no Web site

Irish Police Service (Garda Síochaná), Phoenix Park, Dublin 8; Tel: 01 666 0000, Web site: www.irlgov.ie/garda/angarda

Isle of Man Constabulary, Glencrutchery Road, Douglas IM2 4RG; Tel: 01624 631212.

Ministry of Defence Police, Wethersfield, Braintree, Essex CM7 4AZ; Tel: 01371 854174, Web site: www.mod.uk/mdp

Royal Borough Parks Police Service, The Stable Yard, Holland Park, Ilchester Place, London W8 6LU; Tel: 020 7471 9811, Web site: www.rbkc.gov.uk

Royal Botanic Gardens Constabulary, The Royal Botanic Gardens, Kew, Richmond, Surrey TW9 3AB; Tel: 020 8332 5121, Web site: www.rbgkew.org.uk

Royal Parks Constabulary, The Old Police House, Hyde Park, London W2 2UH; Tel: 020 7298 2000, Web site: www.royalparks.org.uk

Special Constabulary; Hotline: 0845 608 3000; Web sites: www.special-constabulary.com and www.specialconstables.gov.uk

States of Jersey Police, PO Box 789, Jersey JE2 3ZA; Tel: 01534 612612, Web site: www.police.gov.je

UK Atomic Energy Constabulary, Building F6, Culham Science Centre, Abingdon, Oxfordshire OX14 3DB; Tel: 01235 463757, Web site: www.ukaea.org.uk/ukaeac

MISCELLANEOUS

Association of Chief Police Officers, 25 Victoria Street, London SW1H 0EX; Tel: 020 7227 3434, Web site: www.acpo.police.uk

Centrex, Central Police Training and Development Authority, Tel: 01256 602 100, Web site: www.centrex.police.uk

Civil Service & Local Appointments Commissioners, Chapter House, 26/30 Abbey St Upper, Dublin 1; Tel: 01 858 7400, Web site: www.publicjobs.gov.ie

Consensia Partnership, Recruitment Branch, Room 12A, Lisnasharragh, 42 Montgomery Road, Belfast BT6 9LD

Garda College, Templemore, Co. Tipperary, Eire; Tel: 01 666 0000, Web site: www.garda.ie/angarda/college

High Potential Police Development Scheme, 2nd Floor, Allington Towers, 19 Allington Street, London SW1E 5EB; Tel: 020 7035 5049

Metropolitan Police Authority, 10 Dean Farrar St, London SW1H 0NY; Tel: 020 7202 0202, Web site: www.mpa.gov.uk

Metropolitan Police Recruitment Hotline: 0845 727 2212

National Criminal Intelligence Service; Web site:www.ncis.gov.uk

National Police Recruitment; Hotline: 0845 608 3000; Web site: www.policecouldyou.co.uk

Police Federation, 15/17 Langley Road, Surbiton, Surrey KT6 6LP; Tel: 020 8335 1000, Web site: www.polfed.org

Police Superintendents' Association, 67A Reading Road, Pangbourne, Berkshire RG8 7JD; Tel: 0118 984 4005, Web site: www.policesupers.com

Scottish Police College, Tulliallan Castle, Kincardine, Fife, FK10 4BE; Tel: 01259 732000, Web site: www.tulliallan.police.uk

Appendix

Examples of numerical and verbal reasoning tests

The new assessment and selection process will be completed in 2004. As described in Chapter 2 applicants will be expected to sit both a numerical reasoning test and a short verbal reasoning test. The tests provided here are a small sample of those published in *How to Pass the Police Recruitment Test* by Harry Tolley, Catherine Tolley, William Hodge (Kogan Page, £9.99, 0 7494 4192 5; forthcoming).

NUMERICAL REASONING TEST

The numerical reasoning test will be presented as a multiple-choice test and aims to test basic numeracy skills. Calculators will not be allowed so candidates are advised to try these practice tests without one.

The number problems given as examples below area are aimed at assessing ability in addition, subtraction, multiplication and division. The answers are given at the end of this section.

Test 1

How much money would it cost to buy seven loaves of bread at 52p a loaf?

A	B	C	D	E
£3.44	£3.54	£3.64	£3.74	£3.8
☐	☐	☐	☐	☐

Test 2

If I pay £4.56 for a tin of paint and 85p for a brush, how much will I have spent in total?

A	B	C	D	E
£5.31	£5.41	£5.51	£5.61	£5.71
☐	☐	☐	☐	☐

Test 3

A car park holds 550 cars when it is full. How many cars does it hold when it is half full?

A	B	C	D	E
1100	250	55	275	350
☐	☐	☐	☐	☐

Test 4

My bus journey to the station takes 35 minutes and my train journey then takes 55 minutes. How long does my journey take in total?

A	B	C	D	E
1½ hours	1¼ hours	70 min	45 min	85 min
☐	☐	☐	☐	☐

Test 5

Out of 13,750 people in a football stadium, 10 per cent are season ticket holders. How many people do not have a season ticket?

A	B	C	D	E
1,375	1,775	10,750	12,375	15,125
☐	☐	☐	☐	☐

Test 6

Each pack of tiles contains enough tiles to cover 4 sq metres. How many packs of tiles are needed to cover a floor, which measures 40 metres by 40 metres?

A	B	C	D	E
440	20	200	40	400
☐	☐	☐	☐	☐

Test 7

A survey samples 1 out of every 9 households. Out of 117 households, how many would be sampled?

A	B	C	D	E
10	11	12	13	14
☐	☐	☐	☐	☐

Test 8

Four streets have the following number of houses in them: 18, 23, 41 and 37. What is the average number of houses per street?

A	B	C	D	E
29.75	31.75	33	37.5	119
☐	☐	☐	☐	☐

Test 9

A motorist is travelling at 72.5 mph in an area where the speed limit is 50 mph. By how much is the driver exceeding the speed limit?

A	B	C	D	E
20.5mph	22.5mph	52.5mph	70.5mph	120.5mph
☐	☐	☐	☐	☐

Test 10

How many 15-litre drums are needed to fill a 450-litre tank?

A	B	C	D	E
30	25	15	5	3
☐	☐	☐	☐	☐

VERBAL LOGICAL REASONING TEST

In this test you are given a set of descriptions of imaginary events (or 'scenarios'), which resemble those encountered by police officers in the course of their duties, together with additional facts, which are known about them. In each case they are followed by a number of conclusions, which might be derived from the information provided. Your task is to evaluate each of the conclusions given, and then, in the light of the evidence, decide if:

A.   The conclusion is *true* given the situation described and the facts that are known about it.

B.   The conclusion is *false* given the situation described and the facts that are known about it.

C.   It is *impossible to say* whether the conclusion is true or false given the situation described and the facts that are known about it.

In order to get a better idea of what you have to do, take a look at the following examples:

▪   study the information provided;

▪   evaluate each of the five conclusions;

▪   using a pencil, mark your answer A, B or C in the answer boxes;

▪   check your answers against those provided at the end of this appendix.

In order to do well in verbal logical reasoning tests, therefore, you have to be able to study the text provided, to extract relevant information from it and having done so be able to reason logically about it – and to do all that under test conditions. To that end, you should try to use the practice test provided in this chapter to develop your ability to:

▪   read the text quickly, making a mental note of what happened, who was involved and when and where the events occurred;

▪   get a sense of what is relevant and what might be irrelevant in the data provided;

▪   keep your eyes open for the 'red herrings', which have been put there to distract you;

▪   avoid making false assumptions, or 'jumping to the wrong conclusions'.

Scan the text in order to find the facts you need in order to work out the correct conclusions.

It should be pointed out that all of the names and situations used in the examples of verbal logical reasoning tests in this chapter are fictitious, consequently any resemblance they may bear to real persons, places or events is coincidental.

Test 1

At 19.05 on 12 December there was a loud explosion in 2, Bathurst Street. A woman and child managed to escape from the house unhurt, but the ensuing fire claimed the lives of an elderly man and young baby. It is also known that:

▧ John Watts aged 91 owned 2 Bathurst Street.

▧ A smell of gas had been reported at 15.00 on 12 December from 2 Bathurst Street.

▧ At 20.30 on 12 December the police informed Fred Watts of the death of his father.

▧ Fred Watts works nightshift at a local factory.

▧ Fred Watts is a divorcee.

1. The explosion at 2 Bathurst Street on 12 December was due to a leaking gas pipe.

2. Fred Watts was married to the woman who escaped safely from the explosion.

3. The police took less than two hours to find the house-owner's son.

4. A gas leak could have been the reason for the explosion.

5. John Watts was not a grandfather.

Test 2

At 02.20 on Sunday, a four-wheel-drive vehicle plunged over the edge of a steep mountain pass and burst into flames as it reached the valley bottom. There were no survivors. The sole victim has been identified as Mr John Joseph Broon of Muckty, a village 3 km from the scene of the accident. It is also known that:

- John Broon was an alcoholic who had sought help from Alcoholics Anonymous.

- John Broon had been at the local pub from 6 pm on Monday to 02.10 on Tuesday.

- John Broon had a wife and two children.

- The barperson at the local pub had served John all night.

- The drive from the local pub to John's house took 15 minutes along a narrow twisty road, which hugged the mountainside.

- A dead sheep was found on the side of the valley, 100 metres from where the car left the road.

1. John Broon was on his way home when he was killed.

2. John Broon had swerved to miss a sheep on the narrow road and had gone over the edge of the valley side.

3. John Broon was the only person in the car when it crashed.

4. The alcohol content of John Broon at 02.20 would have been over the legal limit.

5. John Broon had eaten a large supper at home with his wife and two children at 21.00 on Monday.

Test 3

The new sports club at Dolchem was vandalised on Friday evening after the boy scouts had finished their weekly meeting in the new hall. Damages are expected to be over £4,000. It is also known that:

▓ The Parish Council was in debt after the construction of the new sports club.

▓ Local teenagers opposed the proposal to charge people to use the club's facilities.

▓ The boy scouts have abandoned the old village hall where they used to have their meetings.

▓ There is a high level of youth unemployment in Dolchem.

▓ Witnesses saw a group of five youths running away from the club at 21.30 on Friday.

▓ Spray cans were used on the club walls, liquid paint and faeces were deposited on the floor and windows were smashed.

1. Five young men were seen running away from the club at 21.30 on Friday.

2. The boy scouts are willing to pay to use the new club.

3. The youth of Dolchem had a motive to vandalise the new sports club.

4. The Parish Council had profited from the construction of the new sports club.

5. The idea of charging people to use the new sports facilities had caused some opposition among the younger members of the community.

Test 4

A night watchman was attacked when a fuel depot in Netherwich was broken into on 24 December and cash was stolen. A police spokesman said that Bill Sykes, a local man, had been taken into custody on 26 December, and was 'assisting them with their enquiries' into what could only be described as a 'violent but amateurish crime'. It is also known that:

- Bill Sykes has been living with his girlfriend Nancy.

- Bill Sykes is the owner of a bull terrier dog.

- The night watchman was distracted by the barking of a dog, and was hit over the head from behind.

- Sykes is already under a community service order for demanding money with menace from his estranged wife.

- Since 31 December Mrs Sykes has complained that her husband had been pestering her to provide him with an alibi for the 24 December.

1. Bill Sykes broke into the fuel depot and hit the night watchman over the head.

2. Sykes stole the money from the fuel depot to give to his wife.

3. Sykes has already been given an opportunity to avoid a custodial sentence.

4. Sykes's girlfriend Nancy hit the night watchman over the head.

5. The burglary was well planned and professionally executed.

Test 5

At 16.05 on Sunday 3 June, an elderly man was found dead in Cuthbert Park. His right-hand wrist had been slashed. The park-keeper had seen a young man running out of the park at 15.30. The following facts are known:

▨ The park had been shut for major landscape changes.

▨ The young man was employed by the landscape contractors and worked in the park.

▨ The dead man had been diagnosed with terminal cancer on Friday 1 June.

▨ The landscape contractors do not work on Sundays.

▨ The park-keeper is profoundly deaf.

▨ A sharp knife with a 16-centimetre blade was found 100 metres from the dead body.

▨ The victim was right-handed.

1. The park-keeper heard a scream from inside the park at 15.25 on Sunday 3 June.

2. The victim may have committed suicide.

3. The young man seen running out of the park had just clocked off from his work with the landscape contractors.

4. The knife found 100 metres from the body had been used to slash the victim's wrist.

5. The victim had been mugged and stabbed by the young man.

Appendix

ANSWERS TO NUMERICAL REASONING TESTS

1: C   2: B
3: D   4: A
5: D   6: E
7: D   8: A
9: B   10:A

ANSWERS TO VERBAL LOGICAL REASONING TESTS

Test 1
1: C; 2: C; 3: A; 4: A; 5: B

Test 2
1: C; 2: C; 3: A; 4: C; 5: B

Test 3
1: C; 2: C; 3: C; 4: B; 5: A

Test 4
1: C; 2: C; 3: A; 4: C; 5: B

Test 5
1: B; 2: A; 3: B; 4: C; 5: C

Index

Also published by Kogan Page

How to Pass the Police Initial Recruitment Test
Ken Thomas, Catherine Tolley & Harry Tolley, 2004, 0 7494 4192 5

Careers and Jobs in IT
David Yardley, 2004, 0 7494 4245 X

Careers and Jobs in Nursing
Linda Nazarko, 2004, 0 7494 4249 2

Careers and Jobs in the Media
Simon Kent, 2004, 0 7494 4247 6

Careers and Jobs in Travel and Tourism
Verité Reily Collins, 2004, 0 7494 4205 0

The A–Z of Careers and Jobs
Jan Poynter, 2004, 0 7494 4206 9

Choosing Your Career
Sally Longson, 2004, 0 7494 4103 8

Great Answers to Tough Interview Questions
Martin Yate, 2001, 0 7494 3552 6

How to Pass Numeracy Tests
Harry Tolley & Ken Thomas, 2000, 0 7494 3437 6

Readymade CVs
Lynn Williams, 2004, 0 7494 4274 3

Readymade Job Search Letters
Lynn Williams, 2004, 0 7494 4277 8

Test Your Own Aptitude
Jim Barrett, 2003, 0 7494 3887 8

The above titles are available from all good bookshops. To obtain further information, please contact the publisher at the address below:

Kogan Page Limited
120 Pentonville Road
London N1 9JN
United Kingdom
Tel: +44 (0) 20 7278 0433
Fax: +44 (0) 20 7837 6348
www.kogan-page.co.uk